Advance Praise for *Millennials with Kids*

"A great read! Providing a fresh look at the American family, this book is chock-full of strategy, but written in a way that makes you feel like you are grabbing a coffee with the authors. *Millennials with Kids* is both informative and entertaining and tells the story of a changing market influenced by the most powerful generation to date."

—Julia Kanouse, Vice President of Marketing, National Restaurant Association

"Could not put this book down! *Millennials with Kids* offers a new look into a generation that approaches parenting in a completely different way. You will finish this book knowing how to effectively engage and inspire these young parents."

—Patty Fair, Brand and Consumer Insights Expert, Whole Foods

"Embracing new marketing strategies like the Brand Atom will be imperative for businesses wanting to succeed in the digital era. Jeff and Marissa have developed new schemas that will not only help us to better understand the millennial parent cohort but will also guide the future of marketing. Great read for those invested in making an impact in our market today."

—Jenny Rooney, Editor of CMO Network, Forbes

"*Millennials with Kids* should be required reading for marketers and executives looking to understand this young, influential segment. It busts many myths and provides rich frameworks and case studies that show what is and isn't effective with this demographic."

—Sucharita Mulpuru-Kodali, Retail Analyst, Forrester Research

"There were numerous times throughout the book where I thought, 'Wow, this could be me. I eat there; I buy that; I shop like that; that's important to me' and the list goes on. As both a millennial mom and an Executive Chef at Applebee's, this book is a must-read for brands looking to connect with other 'mompreneurs' like myself."
—Jessica James, Executive Chef, Applebee's,
and writer for RealFamilyKitchen.com

"As we are reimagining ways the National Turkey Federation can connect with modern consumers, *Millennials with Kids* could not be more timely. This book has helped guide our vision and strategy for connecting with millennial families of the future."
—Joel Brandenberger, President,
National Turkey Federation

"Fromm and Vidler dish up much more than interesting food-for-thought in *Millennials with Kids*. If you or your firm have an appetite to capitalize on the many opportunities represented by the massive millennial market, their book serves up a veritable feast of rich and actionable insights."
—Bradley (Woody) Bendle, Consumer Experience &
Insights Expert, Payless ShoeSource Worldwide

"In *Millennials with Kids*, Jeff and Marissa have created a narrative, peppered with real strategy and tangible takeaways, that explains the shifting paradigm of parenthood in the digital age. It is a must-read for marketers trying to reach this influential and ever-evolving generation."
—Stephanie Sladkus, Publisher, People
StyleWatch at Time Inc.

"The ideas and strategies in *Millennials with Kids* enabled us to improve our retail and marketing strategies to ensure more of our premium treats made it to the pet parents who love our brand."
—Scott Ragan, President, Three Dog Bakery

"Book is long on actionable insights . . . easy-to-follow case studies and a few marketing models that break the old-school rules."

—Jim Elms, Chief Executive Officer, Initiative

"*Millennials with Kids* is a great resource to better understand an important subset of an increasingly influential driver of consumer spending. Brand marketers, executives, and investors who read this book will gather key insights into who millennial parents are, what motivates them, and how influential they can be to achieving business results."

—Steph Wissink, Senior Research Analyst, Piper Jaffray

"The transition from 'con'sumer to 'pro'sumer is profound and represents the confluence of all the big shifts we see in connectivity, technology, and cultural consciousness. *Millennials with Kids* captures the importance of these shifts and offers both substantial guidance and encouraging examples to help us confidently navigate a transforming society."

—Nancy Giordano, Applied Futurist and Founder, Play Big Inc. and Cultural Acupuncture

"*Millennials with Kids* is a true testament to how quickly the market changes. The Millennials we thought we knew are now parents and are viewing brands through an entirely different lens. Jeff and Marissa do a wonderful job staying ahead of trends and providing the most actionable tips and tricks to keep up with this constantly changing generation."

—Neeli Bendapudi, Dean, University of Kansas School of Business

"A complete decoding of this enigmatic generation would take volumes, but the Turing-esque cryptography orchestrated by Fromm in his second work provides great insight into the real messages being delivered behind the behaviors of Millennial parents."

—Chris Carlisle, Vice President & General Manager, Jarden Home Brands

"*Millennials with Kids* gives me tools and actionable examples to drive engagement in a digital, social and mobile world that's constantly changing. And most importantly gives me insight into one of the most influential demographics in our society today."

—Dave Finnegan, CIO/VP Tech and Interactive, The Orvis Company

"Grounded in research, *Millennials with Kids* investigates the changing mindsets of young adults as they take on more responsibilities and start families for the first time. Jeff and Marissa explore what it truly means to be a millennial parent, and help bring light to a generation that we once considered to be an enigma."

—Olga Osminkina-Jones, Vice President Marketing Danone Waters of America

millennials with kids

marketing to this powerful and
surprisingly different generation
of parents

JEFF FROMM AND MARISSA VIDLER

⁊AMACOM

AMERICAN MANAGEMENT ASSOCIATION

New York • Atlanta • Brussels • Chicago • Mexico City • San Francisco
Shanghai • Tokyo • Toronto • Washington, D.C.

Bulk discounts available. For details visit: www.amacombooks.org/go/specialsales
Or contact special sales: Phone: 800–250–5308 • Email: specialsls@amanet.org
View all the AMACOM titles at: www.amacombooks.org
American Management Association: www.amanet.org

Library of Congress Cataloging-in-Publication Data

Fromm, Jeff.
  Millennials with kids : marketing to this powerful and surprisingly different generation of parents / Jeff Fromm and Marissa Vidler.
      pages cm
  Includes bibliographical references and index.
  ISBN 978-0-8144-3658-5 (hardcover : alk. paper) — ISBN 978-0-8144-3659-2 (ebook) 1. Young adult consumers—Attitudes. 2. Target marketing. 3. Parents. 4. Generation Y. I. Vidler, Marissa. II. Title.
  HF5415.332.Y66F763 2015
  658.8—dc23
                              2015009454

About AMA

American Management Association (www.amanet.org) is a world leader in talent development, advancing the skills of individuals to drive business success. Our mission is to support the goals of individuals and organizations through a complete range of products and services, including classroom and virtual seminars, webcasts, webinars, podcasts, conferences, corporate and government solutions, business books, and research. AMA's approach to improving performance combines experiential learning—learning through doing—with opportunities for ongoing professional growth at every step of one's career journey.

Printing number

10 9 8 7 6 5 4 3 2 1

CONTENTS

FOREWORD

As the CEO of Beazer Homes, I have had my eye on the Millennial generation for several years. You simply can't be in a consumer-facing business without acknowledging that we face an unprecedented test: Understand, interact with, and ultimately meet the needs of these Millennials, or run the risk of being passed by the most important demographic wave of the century. It is not an exaggeration to say that these enigmatic and yet powerful young adults hold most consumer markets in the palms of their hands. Their behaviors and preferences will impact the future of today's most successful brands even as they embrace new and disruptive brands.

After reading *Marketing to Millennials*—coauthored by Jeff —I felt as if I had a reasonable grasp on the Millennial generation. I had a better sense of what they were looking for, how they were looking, and what they expected to happen when they found "it." This led to actionable and measurable strategies we put to work in our company.

Then those pesky Millennials had to go and grow up and start their own families and change the rules . . . again.

We were told in *Marketing to Millennials* that 18- to 34-year-olds were the enigma generation. Now they are rapidly becoming the socially pragmatic generation, crowdsourcing everything from baby food to babysitters as they seek out businesses to help them streamline their increasingly busy lives.

Millennials with Kids is an entertaining and widely informative look into the mindset of our economy's newest parents. As explained in the book, these young parents are looking at businesses and brands through a more practical lens. Instead of asking "How can you solve my problems?," these Millennial parents are looking for the tools to address problems *themselves*. This is a highly independent generation, and they simply do not rely on their predecessors the same way Baby Boomers did when they started families.

While the saying "It takes a village to raise a child" is still true today, we must recognize that the village has grown by the 500 friends the average Millennial now has on Facebook. And that's before taking into account the other social and crowdsourced resources today's parents are relying on. As digital natives, these Millennial moms and dads are researching and connecting with brands across dozens of different platforms, primarily from their mobile devices. If you don't understand why they do the things that they do, then you won't be positioned to participate in their activities.

While all of that is a bit daunting to me as a business leader (and also a humbling revelation about my own parenting efforts), Jeff and Marissa have boiled down the most important things to know about Millennial parents into digestible and actionable insights. In our market today, it is "keep up or keep out," and this book provides you with the tools not just to keep up but also to get ahead.

I have known Jeff for more than 30 years. He has always been at the forefront of predicting consumer trends that most marketers don't discover until it is too late. He and Marissa have put together a Millennial parents' guidebook that explains not just what they are doing but also why they are doing it and how you should adjust to increase engagement and, ultimately, your success. You will not want to put this book down, but when you do I guarantee it will be filled with notes and dog-eared pages—either in writing or on your e-book platform.

Allan Merrill
CEO, Beazer Homes

ACKNOWLEDGMENTS

Creating this book was a big endeavor, and we had amazing collaboration.

Marissa Vidler, my coauthor, brought years of marketing research experience, writing talent, marketing wisdom, and a passion that never faded. To all my business partners, thank you for your support and guidance. Leah Swartz interviewed numerous sources and wrote and rewrote entire sections of the book before, during, and after her graduation from the University of Kansas—what a champ. Greg Vodicka worked to improve new business models, while Chris Dickey helped turn Big Data into useful and actionable marketing strategies. David Gutting was actively involved in the original qualitative and quantitative research we conducted and made significant contributions to the early development of our thesis, structure, and ideas. David Weaver and Joe Cox made insightful suggestions as we deconstructed traditional marketing strategies and reimagined models that will guide the marketing industry in the future. Jordan McCormack and Brendan Shaughnessy were involved throughout the entire process and were ready to help with copy review and offer their support whenever needed. Finally, Jeff King gave us his total confidence and emotional intelligence. Thank you all!

To my friends at Consumer Orbit, Staci Kassen and Jay Huckabay, who burned the midnight oil to help build behavior-based orbits that were deduced from analyzing 11 million U.S. Millennial households that already have children. Ryan Barker and BERA Brand Management also played a crucial role in our reimagination of Millennial Brand Love and the brand value equation. In addition, Woody Bendle and Rebecca Zogbi performed a comprehensive and insightful review of our final work that significantly improved the product.

We appreciate the support of the AMACOM team, including Ellen Kadin, Irene Majuk, and Rosemary Carlough.

For all these contributions, Marissa and I are grateful.

In addition, I want to recognize and thank Rhonda, Laura, Abby, and Scott as well as my parents, Bill and Bernie, and my brothers, Andy and Dan, for their ongoing love and support. Marissa would like to thank her husband, Andrew, for his love and unwavering support, not to mention his patience for the countless weekends and evenings lost to writing. She'd also like to thank her parents, Cindy and Michael, sister Megan, and all of her friends, whose support keeps her going every day.

Jeff Fromm

Introduction

The year is 2035. Millennials, who have since rejected the term "Millennial" as too youthful, now call themselves the "Pragmatist" generation and are in the throes of middle age. Wisdom and practicality have replaced their once carefree and adventurous ways. Their status as the most tech-savvy generation has long since been overtaken by their own offspring, who are now teenagers and young adults themselves.

When Millennials were younger, they created their own unique language, digital shorthand, and developed social networks that connected them across countries and continents, giving a global perspective to what was once a small world. As they grew up and entered the work world, their influence shifted from being participative consumers to being inventive brand designers, marketers, and ambassadors.

For many Millennials and their children, dependence on the manufacturing, food, and retail organizations that were a necessity for earlier generations is no more. Living off the grid and growing your own food are the norm, and DIY and on-demand manufacturing are commonplace thanks to the 3-D printer in almost every home. This has made a ghost town of what was once a nation with a thriving capitalist economy. Many of the tombstones memorializing former businesses are etched with the same epitaph: "Destroyed by Millennials. If only there had been a book . . ." Only the organizations that invested in learning about Millennials, especially as they matured and started families of their own, survived and thrived.

It is possible that this is an exaggeration, though we won't know for sure for a few more decades. We do not have a crystal ball that can predict the future of organizations. (If we did, this book would cost a lot more.) What we can say with complete certainty is that the world is changing, largely led and influenced by the Millennial generation and its unprecedented impact on the tastes, attitudes, and culture of older generations. As members of this generation mature and impose their values, attitudes, and behaviors onto their own children, the organizations that don't invest in understanding who these consumers are now and who they will be as they mature may want to begin shopping around for tombstones.

If this fabricated story about the collapse of Western civilization doesn't convince you of the sheer power of Millennials, maybe the facts will. With more than 78 million Americans born between 1977 and 1996, Millennials make up approximately one-quarter of the U.S. population, surpassing Baby Boomers (born 1946 to 1964) and eclipsing Generation X (1965 to 1976) three times over. The utter size of this generation is enough for most organizations to take notice, but, as they say, size isn't everything.

The buying power of Millennials is immense and diversified. Millennials already account for an annual $1.3 trillion in consumer spending in the United States,[1] which will only continue to grow as

THERE ARE 3 MILLENNIALS FOR EVERY GEN XER IN THE U.S.

they mature in their careers and become more affluent. But it's not just the money they spend; it's the influence they wield that impacts how other generations spend their money. Millennials are the largest population in our market today—there are roughly three Millennials for every Generation Xer in the United States.

If you haven't already read *Marketing to Millennials: Reach the Largest and Most Influential Generation of Consumers Ever*, by Jeff Fromm and Christie Garton (AMACOM, 2013), we highly recommend it. Really, it's a great read. Offering a deep dive into the Millennial Mindset™—how Millennials live, think, and shop—*Marketing to Millennials* unveils a number of important insights about this generation that you should know before reading this book, including that Millennials:

- Are some of the earliest "digital natives"

- Are interested in participating in your marketing

- Are known as content creators and users

- Crave adventures—often "safer" adventures

- Strive for a healthy lifestyle

- Seek peer affirmation

- Are hooked on social media in much the same way that older generations are hooked on e-mail at work

- Are not a homogeneous cohort

- Embrace authentic cause marketing and align to brands with a purpose

- Are in many ways similar to older generations

What about what's next for Millennials, as they grow, mature, and start families? While these insights and strategies can be applied across the board to this generation, some important differences between Millennial parents and those who are not parents emerged during the research for this book. Most significant of these differences is the shift toward pragmatism. Of course, it isn't news that young adults who become parents tend to become more grounded as their priorities shift to keeping this little person alive. This story is as old as time. So why can't marketers look to past generations and use those strategies to target Millennials as they move to the next life phase? The answer is simple: Millennials' defining characteristics don't just disappear when their children are born. They are not disconnecting from their smartphones, losing compassion for causes they once cared about, or shunning adventure. Like Millennials without kids, parents are strongly defined by the generational traits that have set the Millennial population apart from everyone else. However, they are finding new ways to use technology to streamline the trials and tribulations of parenthood, refocusing their support on more local causes, and finding adventure closer to home that is inclusive of their children.

The differences that emerged from the research that supported *Marketing to Millennials* was enough to wet our whistles about Millennial parents and left us hungry for more. This led to a custom research effort incorporating a quantitative survey among Millennial parents and a Big Data application, which we've summarized in this book. (If you are interested in the long-form report, just go to http://www.millennialmarketing.com/research.)

This book is designed to be an easy and enjoyable read from which you'll walk away with a better understanding of who Millennials are becoming as they mature and settle down and how to best reach them. Unlike so many business books before ours, we don't want your only takeaway from this book to be how very smart (we think) we are, having bored you to tears with charts and graphs. Rather, we want you to take away key insights, strategies, and thought starters that show your colleagues just how smart *you* are for having read this book. Everyone wins.

Each chapter highlights new marketing strategies that are effective when you are reaching out to Millennials as they step into this new life phase—parenthood. While the primary focus of this book is Millennial parents, the majority of our findings and research shows that Millennial women today are still the primary decision makers for household purchases (very much like Generation X and Boomer households). We found that Millennial moms have a strong presence in the consumer economy today and are greatly influencing the way brands are connecting with young families. We feature a variety of case studies that highlight brands that are doing it right and brands that are doing it wrong when it comes to campaigns that engage Millennials and, by extension, Millennial parents. And don't forget, Millennial parents are people, too, which is why all examples aren't just about diapers and baby products (though there are some). There is loads of data (don't worry, not the boring kind) that supports our findings and insights. At the end of each chapter, we provide key takeaways that highlight the most important information that can be applied to your own organization.

Throughout this book we challenge you to unlearn and reimagine what you thought you knew about marketing to Millennial parents. We break down traditional models that have been a part of the marketing industry for decades and create new Millennial-driven models that represent brands as living organisms. We believe that these new systems of thinking will inspire and influence the way you view and market your brand.

We've peppered this book with interviews from executives who market to Millennial parents, interviews with actual Millennial parents, and case studies, to keep things interesting and applicable. You may laugh; you may cry; you may learn something. Or you may not. We can't say for sure, but we guarantee that we have done our best to provide you with the most insightful and thought-provoking information. These insights can be used not only to better your consumer engagement strategies, but also to help you make your brand stronger overall.

CHAPTER 1

Who Are They Now?

Why is our culture so intrigued with the very idea of generations? It stems in part from the rise of mass society—a relatively recent phenomenon—and how easy it is for a group to share common experiences. Baby Boomers bonded over TV culture, rock 'n' roll, Motown, opposition to the Vietnam War, and the go-go 1980s. Decades later, Millennials bonded over the rise of the Internet, Facebook, and the tumultuous first decade of the twenty-first century—9/11, two wars, and the Great Recession.

Generational divides also stem from the natural rivalry that exists between those who are older and those who are younger. The generation gap has been fueled for decades by stories starting with the phrase "Back in my day," followed by some unbridled narrative explaining how the younger generation has life much easier and is far too unappreciative. It happens in every era. Socrates famously complained about the lazy youth of Athens (Aristotle being one of those "good-for-nothings") and believed they would spell doom for Greek society. Centuries later, the Greatest Generation, whose defining moment of youth was landing on Omaha Beach, looked at their Baby Boomer, hippie-loving children with alarm as they attended Woodstock and defined the Summer of Love. Now those same Boomers cannot understand how their entitled children cannot leave their homes without their smartphones and tablets and prefer texting to personal calls. Fortunately, their kids (whom we all know as the Millennials) are growing up and leaving their selfishness behind them.

In fact, there is an epidemic raging through the Millennial generation, and it seems to be unstoppable. All signs point to the continual spread of this epidemic until the vast majority of the Millennial population is affected. Once exposed, *everything* changes—in a heartbeat. What could be so contagious, so powerful, so life-altering? *Parenthood.*

About one in four Millennials is a parent already, and in the next ten to fifteen years Millennial women will give birth at the rate of roughly 10,000 per day. Over the next twenty-five years, 80 percent of Millennials will be like every generation before them as they step into their new roles of mom and dad. Our media-saturated culture hasn't yet caught up with this reality. There is still a chronic tendency to report on Millennials as if they were still an exotic species, ahead of the rest of us in technology adaptation and practitioners of all kinds of peculiar habits. This is a myopic view of the generation. The truth about them lies elsewhere.

Parenthood is one dimension of that truth. One of the things that modern brands must come to grips with is that Millennials who are parents act, think, behave, and consume differently than those who are not. Understanding this difference and adapting product, branding, and marketing strategies to appeal to this ever-changing generation could be the dividing line between thriving and crumbling brands in the future marketing landscape. It also means recognizing that the Millennial generation as a whole is, indeed, different, and the differences that have shaped this generation will make it a market group unlike any we have known before. Here are some of the critical differences:

- **The Great Recession hurt them far more than any other age group**. The Millennials are the first since the generation that grew up in the 1930s who have been forced to start their working lives at a time when prosperity remains elusive. That has had a notable effect on how young families are forming and evolving.

- **They've delayed or avoided marriage.** Marriage means household formation and signifies a time when adults settle down and often combine two incomes to achieve shared prosperity in order to start a family. However, according to the Pew Research Center, only 26 percent of Millennials have married so far—that's far below the marriage rate of Gen Xers when they were the same age (36 percent) and that of Baby Boomers (48 percent).[1]

- **The Millennial "monolith" is a myth.** In short, there really is no such thing as a single Millennial outlook. Among Millennial parents, we've identified five distinct—and statistically valid—behavioral segment groupings. These segments, or "orbits," are vastly different from one another and reflect everything from the footloose Millennial stereotype to families that look suspiciously like Ward and June Cleaver. You'll read more about these orbits in Chapter 2.

Getting Older and Wiser

The overall Millennial experience as we have come to understand it looks something like this: Growing up, they were surrounded by a party. Born into the Wolf of Wall Street 1980s and dot-com boom of the 1990s, the prospect of wealth and fulfillment was within reach for all—it was just a matter of loving and believing in yourself and doing what makes you happy. How wonderful for children to be raised during a time when they could do anything they wanted! Then, when they were old enough to enjoy it, someone took the punch bowl away.

By the time Millennials entered young adulthood, the great recession of our time, starting in early 2008, changed the playing field. Jobs were hard to come by. Recent college graduates began competing with experienced workers, who were willing to work for below their pay grade or skill set. This roller-coaster economy, which hasn't quite made its way back up, is one of the reasons that Millennials feel financial pressure to such a great extent. Millennial parents, in particular, feel the pinch. The "Millennials as New Parents" study by Barkley's new Millennial consultancy, FutureCast, revealed that 54 percent of Millennials say it is harder to make ends meet since they became parents.[2] This research also revealed that 48 percent of Millennial parents still believe kids are better off if a stay-at-home mom raises them. So, what do you do when Baby is on the way and both Mom and Dad need to work to make ends meet?

Meet Emily: She is 32 years old and has been married more than ten years, with two young children. Emily and her husband were both gainfully employed when they first met. (In fact, they met at work!) Before the kids came along, they scrimped and saved and bought a home in the Bay Area, about an hour east of their jobs and Emily's in-laws. Their daughter was born shortly after the real estate market went in the tank, leaving them upside down on their mortgage. Emily wanted to stay home with their new daughter, so they made the tough decision to sell the house and move in with Emily's in-laws. Even though Emily had worked hard in her career and knew it would be a difficult sacrifice, she felt strongly about staying home with her daughter and not juggling baby-sitters, nannies, and day care. After their second baby was born, they made another conscious decision that Emily would not work for two years so she could be home with the kids, which left them with only one income and forced them to extend their stay with her in-laws while they saved money for another house. Eventually, they saved enough money and were able to purchase a new home (though they had to stay with the in-laws for another few months while the house was being built).

Finally, years later, they are (quite happily) on their own. Living with the in-laws had its perks, both financially and for child care, but it was often a difficult sacrifice. "We never got ahead financially, which is what we needed to be doing to move where we wanted. At some point, we had to prioritize the kids over work, over money, and over my career for a little while. The balance has shifted back now that the kids are older and slightly more self-sufficient. I'm working full-time and I'm happy with that. I'm focused on my career, but at the time we thought it was more important to prioritize them." Emily's story reminds us that not only are there different segments of Millennial parents (which you'll read more about later in this chapter), but there are many changes that occur when Millennials have kids, some of which are permanent and some that are just another step in their journey.

There are many myths surrounding the Millennials: They are lazy; they are self-absorbed; they are not reaching their full potential. However, one of the most prevalent myths about them is that they are the best-educated and most affluent generation in history. This is simply not true. If we do a comparison, we see that Millennials are actually aligned with the Boomer generation in terms of post–high school education. What has changed drastically since Millennials have come of age is the life road map that has traditionally guided young adults. For previous generations we think of a very linear path: First comes love, then comes marriage, then comes baby in a baby carriage, right? However, many young men and women today are stepping into these new roles without first having completed the laundry list that traditional Boomer parents followed. A large portion of young women are now opting to have children out of wedlock. These single mothers are typically career-driven women who have not found a partner, or are still looking, but do not want to put off motherhood. Many women feel that having a child is incredibly important, and they are not willing to sacrifice that if they have not met their life partner yet. According to the U.S. Department of Health and Human Services, 35 percent of 25- to 29-year-olds and 22 percent of 30- to 34-year-olds who gave birth in 2012 were not

married.[3] So is this all acciden-
tal, or is this a choice? For some,
it is a conscious choice, as many
Millennials deliberately decide
to have babies without first getting married—in essence, they
are willing to delay marriage but
not parenthood.

MYTH

Millennials are the best-educated and most affluent generation in history. Millennials are actually in line with Boomers for post-high school education. They have also accrued more than 1.2 trillion dollars in student debt.

This trend is particularly prevalent among those without a four-year college degree.[4] A recent Pew research study further affirms this trend by revealing a perception shift among Millennials, who ultimately put more weight on the importance of being a good parent (52 percent) than on having a successful marriage (30 percent).[5] Kay S. Hymowitz, William E. Simon Fellow at the Manhattan Institute, suggests that this trend is "not the widespread rejection of marriage; it's not even the record number of thirty something brides and grooms. It's the abandonment of the idea that marriage has anything to do with children."[6] It could also be argued that the decision many young adults are making to have children separate from marriage is a function of the increasing divorce rate combined with the perception that it's easier for women to earn an independent living in today's economy.

For Ann, a single mother to her 5-year-old son, there is no question in her mind that parenting is a priority over marriage. "People come and go as far as boyfriends, but I'll always be his mother and he'll always be my son. Marriage is really not a priority whatsoever. If it happens, it happens, but it's not something I actively pursue. Blood is thicker than water."

Though happily married for ten years and with two kids, Emily also understands why some Millennials value parenthood over marriage. "I was really into getting married when I was younger, but now, if anything were to happen, heaven forbid, and right now we are in a good place, I don't know if I would ever get married again. It just wouldn't be important to me. I can see why people prioritize having kids if that is what is important to them."

Amber, mother of two and married eleven years, echoes Emily's sentiment. "Marriage is hard, but kids love you forever. Kids just have an unconditional love for you. Of course, it's a battle raising them and teaching them right from wrong, but with a spouse, sure—you picked them to be your life partner, but growing together and being on the same page is tough."

Bret, a father of three and husband of eleven years, has a slightly different view from those in the previous stories. Knowing that he couldn't do it all without his wife's support, he places a stronger value on marriage. While many women are happy and willing to begin a family in the absence of traditional marriage, Millennial men show a few more insecurities about becoming fathers without the support of another parent. According to a 2014 DDB study, a majority of Millennial father survey participants feel a significant amount of pressure most of the time when discussing their parenting responsibilities.[7] However, the value Bret puts on marriage is dependent on the role he feels it plays in his ability to be a good father. "I would never say this to my kids, but my relationship with my wife is really, really important, maybe more important than my relationship with my kids. I feel like, without that relationship with her, I wouldn't be a very good father. I'm a better father if I have a good relationship with my wife."

This decision by young adults to enter parenthood based on a nontraditional life path affects the way markets are connecting with these Millennials. It is important to realize that "family" in the United States looks very different today than it did even ten years ago. Messaging to Mom is no longer messaging to the homemaker. Now brands must walk a thin line between engaging the working, single mother and connecting with the stay-at-home, married mother. Both women are equally important to a brand but require different messaging strategies. We are also seeing a significant shift in the role of Dad as Millennial men are becoming first-time fathers. Fatherhood has been changing for decades, largely an outcome of women's evolving and increasing role in the workforce. Dad as breadwinner and Mom as caretaker are no longer the status quo. In analyzing U.S. Census Bureau data, Pew Research has identified that 40 percent of women are the sole or primary source of income for the family, which is up from only 11 percent in 1960.[8] Some of this increase is attributed to single mothers, but almost four in ten (37 percent) are married women. Additionally, there is evidence that in married households the median income is higher when the woman is the breadwinner, reflecting the fact that she frequently has a level of education similar to or higher than that of her husband. Want to learn more about Dad? Don't worry, we will dive into a deeper discussion about his new role in Chapter 6.

Statistics aside, the dynamic of deciding who stays at home with the kids has evolved from an assumption to a discussion. These changing perceptions of marriage and parenthood are Millennial driven and have altered the way society as a whole connects with parents and new families. The Millennial stereotypes of yesterday are vanishing as young adults adapt to a new life stage and style.

American Pragmatism Remix— Millennial Style

When Barkley and FutureCast first published the report on Millennials with the Boston Consulting Group and Service Management Group in 2011, it was titled "American Millennials: Deciphering the Enigma Generation." If there is an overriding lesson in what is happening to this generation as it transitions from young adulthood into parenthood, it's that they are no longer as enigmatic as we once thought and there is a newfound pragmatism about them.

It would be easy for the casual critic to look at this claim—and the trend underlying it—and argue, "So what? Is that any surprise? Aren't you telling us what everyone always finds out when they grow up—that you give up your youthful ways and become responsible?" Yes we are, but that isn't the full story. We all know that happens—always has, always will. Our message is actually quite a bit different.

As they move into parenthood, Millennials are not only changing in the ways kids always do when they grow up, but they also are bringing with them an ideology that we haven't seen in this country for a very long time: a dynamic and refreshed form of good ol'-fashioned American pragmatism.

Pragmatism was the first (and really only) philosophical movement to come out of America. Pragmatism isn't just a lifestyle philosophy; it's a powerful theory that describes how we create truth in our lives and how we should act. In other words, it is a real philoso-phy, one that challenged the Old World ideologies of Europe and was shaped by intellectual giants like John Dewey, who said, "In its simplest form, pragmatism comes down to this: Knowledge should not just describe or reflect reality; it should be used to predict action and to solve problems." None of those European philosophers whose writing put you to sleep had ever said that.

Look at American history and American innovation from the late nineteenth century on and you will see the invisible hand of pragmatic philosophy guiding American life. The United States led the world in concepts such as universal education, suffrage for women, and an unbridled spirit of innovation, giving us the likes of Abraham Lincoln, Henry Ford, and Thomas Edison. By the dawn of the twentieth century, the United States was the richest nation on the planet. Its power and leadership won two world wars, conquered the Great Depression, and sent men to the moon and returned them safely to earth.

But you don't have to be a cynic to recognize that more recent American history hasn't been such an upbeat and glowing story. By and large, Americans have lost faith in institutions of all kinds—the government, big business, even the church. Gallup has been study-ing the confidence that people place in major institutions for more than 40 years, and—aside from the military—the picture is fright-ening. This is true especially when looking more closely at the level of confidence Americans have in banks. Results from a June 2014 survey show that only 10 percent of respondents have a great deal of confidence in their banks.[9] This is down from 17 percent just ten years ago.

What does this tell you if your job is to sell products to the American middle class? For decades you've been selling to a cynical, skeptical public. Maybe that has given you an opportunity—sometimes a favorite brand is a simple pleasure amid so much stress in other areas of life. But there's another truth underneath this: Despite the obvious success of certain brands (Apple, Starbucks, Google, and the like), most of the rest of the U.S. economy has been stuck in neutral for a very long time. Economists on both the left (Paul Krugman) and the right (Tyler Cowen) agree on this. Cowen wrote an acclaimed book, *The Great Stagnation*, which contends that innovation in the U.S. economy mostly came to a halt after about 1973, and that we're fooling ourselves into thinking that innovation is either extensive or real. In another widely praised book, *The Unwinding*, George Packer, a writer for *The New Yorker*, weaves a cultural story that depicts a nation stuck in neutral or even in reverse for the past 30 years, with middle-class life slipping away from people who once took it for granted.

However, in this book we make a prediction: Millennials are going to change things. They're going to stop the slide and lead the restoration of prosperity, which will be based on a new, dynamic form of American pragmatism. And they're going to do it as the most innovative and empowered generation of parents in history.

We base this prediction not just on a hunch. It's a combination of a hard look at the demographics and an understanding of how a new generation of con-

PRAGMATISM

The rejection of the previously held notion that a product, service or even function of thought should describe or mirror reality. Instead, pragmatism is centered on the idea that a product, service or function of thought is an instrument used to predict future actions and solve problems. Essentially, pragmatism is a philosophical approach that assesses everything in terms of a practical application.

sumers is behaving. One of our central ideas is that as parents, the people who will define family life for the next thirty years, Millennials will bring a new kind of democracy to our culture. This won't be just a political democracy, though it will have some of those elements. It will be a democracy that infiltrates every level of commerce, culture, and community. It will be a real and empowering democracy—not one that depends on politicians who live off the influence of big money and fight each other to political death.

This has spawned what we are calling the Democracy of Fairness™. Millennials are highly communal by nature, and they expect equality and fair treatment among genders, races, ages, and other demographic categories. Not to mention that they expect fairness when it comes to brand messaging. What does this mean? It means that brands cannot tell consumers what to do. On a level playing field, everyone has an equal role and Millennial consumers act as brand partners rather than brand targets.

For some years now, marketers have been hearing that they don't really control their brands—consumers do. We are past the point of having to discuss that or prove it. It's a given. The real question is this: *What does it mean?* We have some answers, and some hypotheses, and they are found partly in how this generation is behaving as parents but also in the ways they were raised and in the technologies that took hold during their youth.

Here are a few lessons from the initial research that led to this book. Some of these things are clearly happening, and some are things we believe likely will happen:

1. Millennial parents will instill in their children an
    unprecedented sense of individual tolerance and social

responsibility. This will change our politics and our social interactions considerably.

2. Ethnic diversity will be the new normal, and Hispanic culture will experience a rich coexistence with Anglo and African-American culture. A true melting pot will emerge.

3. A core group of Millennial parents—though by no means all—will set a new standard when it comes to health and nutrition. They will insist on a new level of quality and purity in the products they use.

4. Technology will become largely invisible and tech adoption will happen at an even faster rate (think wearable tech). Devices will, of course, always have their lure, but this generation will take them for granted, just as the *Mad Men* generation took cars with automatic transmissions and homes with air-conditioning for granted. Once this happens, the world will experience the real power of the age of information.

5. Emerging media will stop emerging and simply be our daily media. For some time now we have been living in a very noisy world, where clear signals fight to break through. Look for that to change and for a new media order to take hold.

6. Millennial parents will support brands that reflect their values and that think beyond profit. "Cause branding" will not be a sidebar activity. It will become not only integral to success but also a part of the business model. This type of marketing will probably evolve to a place where the highest-performing brands are "conscious capitalist," which

is the likely Darwinian evolution of cause marketing and branding strategy.

7. They will require brands to solve problems if they are to stay relevant. Usefulness will become the new cool, and Millennial consumers will look to brands that can contribute to their new ideas of pragmatism. Unsupported propositions and storytelling that isn't backed by bold action will not have sustained economic impacts. Marketers might even want to dust off the teachings of Claude Hopkins and Rosser Reeves, both of whom knew how to score simple points and make them stick.

8. They will extend and expand the idea of the "participation economy," forcing brands to constantly work for loyalty and acceptance through interactive campaigns and Content Excellence™. This won't be out of cynicism or cockiness—it will just be the way things are. Monopolists and icons beware.

9. If they can live even a few years without the specter of war and recession, this generation will stare down their adversaries and spark a cycle of growth we haven't seen since the dot-com craze of the late 1990s. One simple reason for this: A larger middle-age generation is coming through again, and that means greater demand. Demand means there is a market for brands that meet the new value equation these Millennial parents seek.

10. In the next few decades they will start having grandchildren, and the cycle will start all over again.

Very few of these points are based on idealism or abstraction. They are real, and they reflect trends that are well documented. Just like their grandparents, the Greatest Generation, who fought World War II, Millennials are coming into family life with experiences and mindsets that represent the tough hand they were dealt during childhood and young adulthood—war, recession, and painfully high unemployment. However, at the same time, they were surrounded by explosive change in technology and media. Just like their grandparents, Millennials are inheriting and helping to create a new world.

The Five Orbits of Millennial Parents

We've said it before, and we'll say it again: *Millennials are not a homogeneous cohort.* Each generation is made up of individuals with demographic and psychographic differences—this was a primary focus of our research. Success will come to those who recognize and embrace this generation's heterogeneity. However, it is still important to analyze consumers through a generational lens because it can provide general guidelines for understanding marketing strategies. Throughout this book we utilize both methods of understanding the Millennial parent demographic—through a very close look at how parents from different orbits interact with brands and how Millennial parents as a whole display generational characteristics that influence their relationships with brands.

In our previous book, *Marketing to Millennials*, we introduced six segments of Millennial consumers: Hip-ennials, Gadget Gurus, Anti-Millennials, Old-School Millennials, Clean-and-Green Millennials, and Millennial Moms. We were particularly intrigued by the Millennial Mom segment, which was described as wealthy, family oriented, and confident. But what about Millennial parents who aren't so wealthy? What about those who prioritized other things in life, such as image, career, or marriage? What about those who weren't quite so confident?

To answer these questions, we took a different approach to segmenting Millennial parents. While segmentation can be a useful way to look at consumers, it can often be challenging to implement, as it requires an extensive list of demographic and psychographic questions and a complex algorithm to assign consumers to the correct segment. That's all before the targeting can even begin! This time, we partnered with Consumer Orbit, a tactical analytics firm, to look at segmentation in a different way. Staci Kassen, Consumer Orbit's executive vice president and chief operations officer, said, "The Millennial Parent segmentation permits us to look at a demographically-defined audience with a behavioral-lens. We have identified preferences, behaviors and motivations for how each household navigates and transacts in their daily life among social and cultural influences." To create this orbit system, which focuses on Millennial parents between the ages of 25 and 34, Consumer Orbit pulled from multiple data sources, accessing billions of data points.

From this effort, five distinct Millennial parent orbits were identified: Family First, Style and Substance, Under Stress, Image First, and Against the Grain. Keep in mind that, unlike with traditional segmentation, demographic data such as income, ethnicity, or marital status are not used to configure the orbits, meaning a concentration of any given demographic is a finding itself. In order to provide the most up-to-date information, FutureCast revisited these orbits in June 2014 to update findings and provide the most recent data available on Millennial parents.

This updated research offered another, even more in-depth look at the difference between Millennial nonparents and Millennial parents. Originally, the research compared Millennial parents against the general population of parents. However, the second time around, the research focused more on finding the key differences between Millennial nonparents and Millennial parents. The results might surprise you:

1. **They may not be as involved in the community as you think they are.** According to the data found by FutureCast and Consumer Orbit, there is a large drop in civic, political, and social commitment between Millennial parents and Millennial nonparents. Before they became parents, 12.5 percent of Millennials belonged to a civic organization. After they became parents, however, that number dropped to a surprising 0.3 percent.

2. **They are not as green as you remember.** One of the key findings of the primary FutureCast Millennial study was that Millennials are a holistically "green" generation, meaning that they care about environmental issues and support brands that uphold green initiatives. Research shows that before Millennials became parents 10 percent belonged to an environmental organization; that number decreased to just 0.2 percent after they had children. The rate at which Millennials recycle also experienced a sharp decline after they became parents. While Millennials

overall still value the environment and green issues,
parents do not have the same capacity for time and
budget commitments as nonparents when it comes to
environmental action. Ultimately, green is good when
the economy is good. If a Millennial parent can afford
to spend time or money on green products or initiatives,
then these things often take a backseat to more pressing
matters such as household necessities and education for
their children.

3. **They are a different kind of conservative.** Millennials
   do not consider "conservative" to be just a political
   outlook. Instead, they see it as a definition of how they
   live their lives. After becoming parents, the number of
   Millennials who described themselves as conservative
   evangelical Christians increased from 9.6 percent to 32.9
   percent However, in what could be considered a political
   conundrum, most Millennial parents and Millennials
   overall considered their political views to be more middle
   of the road.

4. **Millennial parents are more concerned about Internet
   privacy.** After becoming parents, Millennials dropped
   their carefree attitude toward online privacy. According to
   FutureCast research, 29 percent of Millennial parents said
   they used the Internet less because of privacy concerns,
   which is up from 9.8 percent of Millennials who said the
   same thing before they were parents. However, Millennial
   parents were more likely than Millennial nonparents to
   share personal information in order to receive coupons

FIGURE 1–1 Five orbits of Millennial parents.

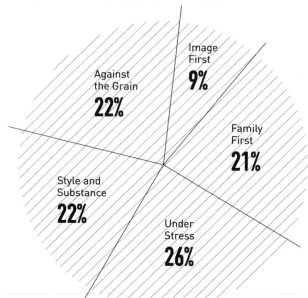

Source: David Gutting and Jeff Fromm, "Millennials as New Parents: The Rise of a New American Pragmatism," Barkley/FutureCast and Consumer Orbit research study, 2013.

from their favorite brands. Budgeting household expenses is worth the risk!

Though these insights are slightly different from what was found in 2013, the orbits themselves did not experience any significant changes. Figure 1–1 breaks down the orbits into an easy-to-understand graph, but, as we have mentioned, each orbit functions slightly differently from the others. In order to better understand the Millennial parent as a consumer, let's delve a little further into the composition of each orbit.

IMAGE FIRST
"I'm Too Sexy"

- 9 percent of Millennial parents
- Confident and ambitious, but sometimes insecure about what other people think about them
- Clothing and fashion are important and often influenced by celebrities
- Want to impress people by being "in the know"
- Skew Hispanic and African-American, high school education, under $60K annual income

Javina loves her two boys, 2 and 4 years of age, and would do anything for them. But becoming a mother didn't change the fact that she cares about how the world views her. It's important to Javina that she present herself to others as clean-cut, sharp, and well put together, but it doesn't just stop with her. "I'm a clean cut person, I'm put together. It makes a statement that if my kids look messy, then that makes me look messy. If my kids don't look put together, then I don't look put together." Brand-name clothing helps her portray herself (and her kids) the way she wants to, but she'll sometimes buy off-brands when money is tight. When it comes to her beauty supplies, however, brand is everything. "I will spend more money on beauty supplies because, with clothing, it can look the same and be a lower price, but with beauty supplies like my skin care, I think it's more important to have a better brand."

This philosophy translates into Javina's work at a specialty bra store that helps women look their best. Working part-time and raising two young boys can be challenging at times, but she shares the responsibility of parenting with her partner of ten years. They met as teenagers and married young, but it just wasn't meant to be. "When we were married, it was like the day that we signed the document, things changed." Marriage wasn't right for them, so they divorced and spent some time apart. Eventually, they got back together and are stronger than ever, with no intention of signing that little piece of legal paperwork again. "If we wake up in the morning and things aren't working, we can get out of this. Every day we wake up and make the choice to be together."

Javina considers herself a technology buff. She likes to have the newest and best gadgets and has everything in her home connected. "My television, my computer, my phone, my tablet. All that stuff. I think that maximizing the use of a phone and tablet can take your time, make it more effective. So I've cut my time for work down by about an hour or two every day."

This is the smallest but most distinct orbit. Millennial parents in this orbit, as the name suggests, are driven largely by their image. They value personal appearance and are usually the first of their friends to know about and act on new trends. This orbit has the highest level of diversity and relatively lower levels of income and education. These parents are very involved in social media and thrive on constant connection to their families, peers, friends, and favorite brands. These are the youngest Millennial parents, but they are the orbit with the oldest children. Many of them are still learning what parenthood means and how to balance their new roles with the challenges that come with having a family.

FAMILY FIRST
"We Are Family"

- 21 percent of Millennial parents
- Kids come first, least likely to sacrifice time with family
- Not interested in style or fashion trends; thrifty; teach kids to respect money
- Use social media to connect with family, not to widen network
- Primarily married, Caucasian, $100K+ annual income

Amanda, 31, has been married for more than nine years and has a 6-year-old daughter and 3-year-old son. Both she and her husband work full-time in professional fields. With the benefit of financial stability, she does not have to work, but she chooses to and she does it for her children. "I felt like I would be a better mother if I could use my education and brain. I can afford my children opportunities they wouldn't have if I wasn't working."

Having been raised Mormons, she and her husband believe in the religion's general values, putting family first, and being good to others. However, resistance to the more historical aspects of the religion, such as the patriarchal system and views on homosexuality, have caused them to look for a new, more progressive church. In the meantime, they send their children to church each week with Grandma.

In this family, the kids come first. "My kids come first because I want them to be first in my life. Work/life balance is something that is important to me and I see the value of placing my children first in my life. Just to watch them grow and see the people that they are going to become and what they are going to do to change the world. Putting them first and giving them a better opportunity to have a successful and happy life."

Amanda doesn't put a high priority on brand-name products when she buys for herself, but she does take brand into consideration when buying for her children. "Brand name products are more important for my kids. I'm looking for that brand recognition, for that trusted brand, for the high quality product so I can be sure I'm taking care of my kids that way." Even though brand name carries some weight, she still seeks out the best deals for these brands by comparing prices on Amazon, looking for deals and coupons, and asking friends about the best place to buy these products.

She also teaches her children about charity and giving to others. When her daughter has toys she no longer plays with, Amanda turns it into a lesson about donating to less fortunate kids. And her charity doesn't end there. After seeing a news story several years ago about a company that recycled car seats, she created a program at her own workplace to recycle them as well.

The Family First orbit looks the most like the families Boomers and many Gen X parents grew up in. Family First is one of the largest orbits and represents a "traditional" family model. Both parents are typically Caucasian, middle class, and married to each other. In this orbit, family is the most important thing. These parents are not as concerned with brand-name products as Image First parents, and they typically lag when it comes to style and fashion trends. The parents in this orbit are still very connected with social media, but they use their networks as a way to communicate with close family and friends.

When they are engaging with brands online, it is usually via their mobile phones and they are typically looking up answers to questions or purchasing products. Family First also has one of the highest concentrations of homemakers, resulting in a lower labor participation rate, even though this is the orbit with the highest level of education.

UNDER STRESS
"She Works Hard for the Money"

- 26 percent of Millennial parents
- Less confident and enthusiastic
- Live paycheck to paycheck
- Put off by food consciousness trend and not interested in style/ fashion
- Mixed marital status, lower income, larger families, under $45K annual income

At 32, Amber has been married for almost eleven years and has two boys, ages 9 and 4. Both Amber and her husband work full-time—he is a pest control specialist and she is a masseuse. Together, they make enough to pay expenses but have not made the progress toward wealth or ownership that they had hoped. Her in-laws, who are in poor health, live with them, bringing the household total to six. This has made it difficult to spread $400 worth of groceries over even just two weeks, let alone to save for a house.

When Amber became pregnant with her first son, she tried reaching out to her mother for parenting advice, but after her mom pushed cloth diapers as religion, Amber quickly found that her advice was outdated, idealistic, and didn't really take Amber's financial stresses into consideration. "She was all about cloth diapers, disposable were new to her. She was trying to push me into a laundry service and I was like, 'that is not going to happen.' For $50 a month, I can get wipes and diapers at Costco, so I politely declined her offer. She was all about being green, and I understand green, but diapers are not the way I'm going to do that."

Being the first of her friends to have a baby, she turned to the Internet to fill the gap when she needed advice. Now, as an experienced mom, her friends turn to her for information and advice. In fact, her sister-in-law is about to have her first child, and Amber has given her advice, even passing along helpful articles from websites like Circle of Moms to help her. Amber also keeps an eye out for product recalls that might affect her friends and family and often posts them online to warn others.

When shopping, low price and long-term value are priorities. She favors Costco, not only for diapers in the early days, but for food and other household items, because the prices are low and she can stock up easily. Target is the go-to for clothes because it is considered "disposable clothing"—it's good enough quality to satisfy her growing children but she can move on without feeling guilty once another growth spurt hits.

She checks Facebook regularly to stay connected to her network of friends, but finds Twitter to be too celebrity oriented. She values the convenience of digital media and uses life maintenance apps to help her organize her schedule. She and her husband sit down with the Google calendar regularly to plan out the month ahead.

Under Stress is another ethnically diverse orbit. It has the second-lowest levels of education and income. Millennial parents in this orbit deal with high levels of stress in regard to unemployment and poor financial situations. This drastically affects their perception of risk taking and adventure. Many parents in this orbit would like to be adventurous but do not have the financial stability to do so. Not surprisingly, this is the group with the least brand consciousness. They pay little attention to brands in product placements and do not notice or place a lot of value on name brands when they encounter them. These parents rarely go shopping for personal items like clothes and accessories, and, when they do, they prefer to shop at specialty stores because they typically carry more brands and have lower prices. The online behavior of Under Stress Millennials is another indicator of how different this orbit is from all the others. A relatively low percentage of Millennial parents in this orbit agreed that the Internet has changed the way they spend their free time. However, they are still very active on their mobile devices and typically rely on their smartphones as a resource when deciding where to go or what to do.

AGAINST THE GRAIN
"I'm Still Standing"

- 22 percent of Millennial parents
- Hardworking, but struggle to move forward
- Adventurous, but don't make time for superficial things
- Use cell phone to connect, not for self-expression
- Primarily Caucasian or Hispanic, high school grad, under $75K annual income

Bryan and his wife had their first child three years ago, just after his wife was laid off from her full-time position. Since then, they've added two more children to their brood: a 2-year-old girl and a 3-week-old bouncing baby boy. Although Bryan has a college degree, he often works several jobs at a time, sometimes seven days a week, in various fields to make ends meet and support his family. After Bryan's wife received a job offer for steady work, they made the decision that he would stay at home and care for the children full-time.

Bryan's fears and anxieties about staying home with his children have nothing to do with concerns about his ability to be a good parent or even about his manhood. Instead, he is worried about letting go of his former self. "I'm excited but nervous. From the time I was 22, I've had a full-time job. To plan to resign from a full-time job and have someone else support me is nerve-wracking. But, I am looking forward to it. It will allow me to go back to school to study nursing. It was an easy decision that I would be the one to stay home with the kids; one of us has to and she makes more money than I do." One thing he remembers from his childhood is that his dad worked hard and wasn't home much, and he's excited to be there more for his own kids.

One of the biggest changes to his lifestyle when he became a parent was the shift from being spontaneous and adventurous to a more structured life. "Before I had kids, I was a lot more carefree and had a lot more time to do what I wanted when I wanted; I was always up to go away for the weekend. Now, life is a lot more structured. It's not about my schedule; it's about the kids' schedule. If I had my way, we would have gone to the park all day today—it's 80 degrees. But, they needed to take their nap, so we had to come home after just a few hours."

Bryan often feels as though his family must live paycheck to paycheck. His wife does most of the shopping for groceries and household items, though that is likely to change as he transitions into his new role of primary caregiver. Bryan primarily uses two websites to stay connected to the world around him: Facebook to keep track of his friends and their lives and Yahoo! for news. Bryan seldom actively participates on social media but still uses Facebook to stay in the know about things that are important to him. Overall, Bryan values the connection he has made through social media and often uses his phone to stay connected and up-to-date.

Millennials in this cohort do not tend to care much for style, fashion, making a statement, or being nonconformists. These Millennials also show little interest in food consciousness and healthfulness, and they lack the upbeat view commonly associated with the Millennial demographic. Against the Grain is overall a "minority majority" group. Parents in this orbit tend to have more kids than parents in any of the other orbits. In general, they are a hardworking group and put great value on brands that stand for more than their bottom line. While this group tends to go "against the grain" in regard to Millennial trends, these parents are nevertheless Millennials, and they display many characteristics that are common to the generation as a whole. They describe themselves as having a sense of adventure, and they actively pursue new and different experiences that they can share with their friends and family. The somewhat lower economic position of parents in this orbit and their lower levels of educational achievement, however, likely explain why these attributes are not more of a focal point for them.

STYLE AND SUBSTANCE
"Say You, Say Me"

- 22 percent of Millennial parents
- Self-assured, confident, and well-informed
- Interested in style and fashion, but practical about it
- Adventurous, with a global and expansive worldview
- Ethnically diverse, some higher education, over $75K annual income

Allison has always been organized and a multitasker, but having kids brought those traits to a whole new level. Both she and her husband work (he full-time and she part-time but always on call), so they depend on technology to manage their household. The primary way they do this is by using a shared Google calendar. Each week, they review the week's calendar to make sure everything is set and identify what needs to be juggled.

Allison's kids use technology, too. They use her iPad for movies in the car or for games at the doctor's office. It keeps her kids engaged and entertained. She doesn't need a vehicle with a DVD player anymore because she has her iPad. Her daughter knows to ask for Pandora by name when she wants to listen to music.

They are as social as they have always been, but it's different now. She is much more particular with her time because it's so limited. "It's easier to say no to people and things that aren't a priority in my life because my kids are a stronger yes. Every time

I agree to something, I'm saying no to my kids." She believes in giving her children choices but starts with giving them good options to choose from. Her daughter tells people that "Mommy and Daddy make the decisions, but I get options."

She is price conscious and often uses Amazon for online purchases, though she has a love-hate relationship with them. "Everything about it I really, truly love except for the fact that I am taking away from shopping at local retailers. I hate that philosophically, but for the age range of my kids and just needing to be home with them and working, Amazon Prime is the greatest thing ever. We're price conscious in every aspect of our lives, but we also want to raise children who are grounded and not too image conscious."

She loves looking at other people's pictures on social media and sometimes posts pictures of her own children, but she is acutely aware that "when you post on social media, you are representing your own brand, so every time I want to post something, I have to think 'Is that what we stand for?'"

These parents constantly put their children before everything and consider their family their top priority. This orbit is the most affluent of Millennials. They have the education and income that have already taken them to a comfortable life and are likely to propel them to the highest level of success among all the orbits. In many ways, the Style and Substance orbit best represents the stereotype of the adventurous, curious, and hyperconnected Millennial. These parents believe in free expression for their children and tend to indulge in nonessential purchases. This is very different from the more structured Family First orbit. Style and Substance Millennials are a media-immersed group in every respect, though not just through digital channels. They rely on the radio and TV to keep them informed and often listen to the radio while they are in the car on the way to work. They use social networks to both connect and expand their world—unlike Family First Millennials, who are more centered on their existing world, using social resources as a practical tool for daily life. Millennial parents in the Style and Substance orbit rely on the Internet to communicate with family and friends and to research products.

Overall, Millennial parents are the first generation to have children who will be a part of a general population shift toward a minority majority. Household income among Millennial parents varies. The Great Recession of 2008 affected many such households, and these Millennials are still feeling heavy financial burdens as they step into their new roles as parents. Only 20 percent of Millennial parents make more than $100,000 per year. One of the greatest myths about Millennials (which we have already dispelled in this book) is that they are the most educated generation. They are, however, in line with Boomers in terms of educational achievement, although overall the United States ranks relatively low on a global scale of average education levels. Figures 1–2 through 1–4 help put these insights into perspective by comparing the different Millennial orbits to each other in regard to ethnicity, income distribution, and education level, respectively.

So You Want to Market to Millennial Parents?

It's time for marketers to change the way they look at Millennials. That means two important changes in viewpoint.

First, marketers should stop looking at Millennials through the lens of stereotypes that have fallen by the wayside. Stop being sur-

FIGURE 1–2   Ethnicity.

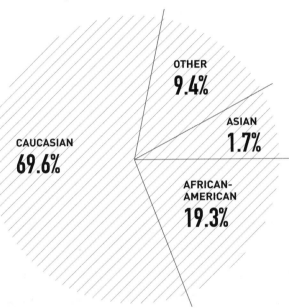

Source: FutureCast and Consumer Orbit Research Study.
Note: 20 percent of Millennial parents who identified as Caucasian, Other, Asian,
or African-American also identified as having Hispanic/Latino/Spanish origin.

prised that Millennials are big users of social media. So is everyone
else. Instead, recognize that what we once called "emerging media"
has emerged and is now dominant. Therefore, emerging media can
now be called traditional media. Marketers must also recognize the
real implication of that. To paraphrase Marshall McLuhan, stop trying to make the new media do the work of the old. The goal is to
master the new media—not just to cater to Millennials, but so you
survive. Additionally, it is imperative that you do not think of Millennials as secondary consumers. Yes, they are living at home with
Mom and Dad a bit longer than people from previous generations

FIGURE 1–3 Income distribution.

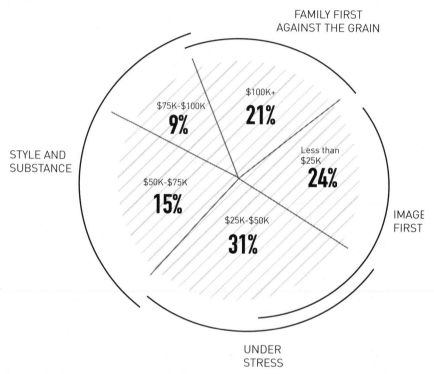

Source: David Gutting and Jeff Fromm, "Millennials as New Parents: The Rise of a New American Pragmatism," Barkley/FutureCast and Consumer Orbit research study, 2013.

did, but that's changing, and they are growing up and settling down just like anyone else.

The second essential change in viewpoint is this: *The Millennial cohort is rapidly becoming the drivetrain of the consumer economy.* In the year 2020, Millennials will range in age from 25 to 42, comprising more than 75 percent of the vital adult 25-to-49 demographic. True, marketing is becoming more about relationships than about mass tar-

FIGURE 1–4   Educational level.

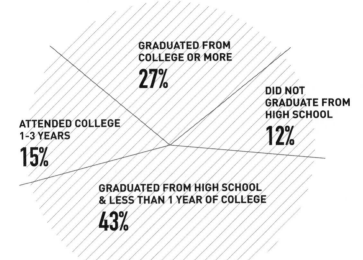

GRADUATED FROM
COLLEGE OR MORE
27%

DID NOT
GRADUATE FROM
HIGH SCHOOL
12%

ATTENDED COLLEGE
1-3 YEARS
15%

GRADUATED FROM HIGH SCHOOL
& LESS THAN 1 YEAR OF COLLEGE
43%

Source: David Gutting and Jeff Fromm, "Millennials as New Parents: The Rise of a New American Pragmatism," Barkley/FutureCast and Consumer Orbit research study, 2013.

geting, but life stage and demographics will still matter. It is this group that will decide where people put down roots, how much they spend on housing and decor, what car brands will rise and fall, what goes in the grocery cart, where people will travel, what electronics are indispensable, how much we invest in education, and who wins and loses elections. And that's just a start! These next few years are the critical ones for shaping strategies to connect with this powerful generation. Now, more than ever, it's time to stop treating them like kids who are an enigma and start treating them like adults who are in charge and make their own decisions and budgets—and who are quite pragmatic.

Here are a few things that marketers of virtually any product or service need to be prepared to confront:

- **Look for a fundamental shift in brand strategy—away from image, away from the ethereal, away from soft claims and "brand narratives."** Will the old-fashioned unique selling proposition (USP) rule? Not at all. Brands will be required to develop a Brand Stand™ and take a position of authority within their market. If all you are building on is emotion, you will likely stand on quicksand.

- **There will be nothing special about digital technology.** In fact, by 2020, it's safe to assume the digital era will be over. For more than twenty years, marketers have carved out individual "digital" strategies and delineated those strategies as something distinct and separate—often forcing nondigital styles into digital shoe boxes. This has been passé for some time. By the next decade, it will be completely irrelevant.

- **Ethnicity, diversity, and family life will rule social behavior.** Millennial women are already giving birth to "minority majority" children. Hispanic, Black, and Asian— all ethnicities in which close family ties are celebrated— already constitute half of the Millennials who have become parents, and they are changing our conception of the "typical" American household.

Now that we have a basic understanding of who Millennial parents are, let's get to the good stuff! This book outlines ways in which marketers should address Millennials now that they have reached a new life stage. We break down and reconstruct traditional engagement models in order to better connect with a new generation of brand partners, who are completely redefining the participation economy as we know it.

CHAPTER 1: KEY TAKEAWAYS

↻ **Many Millennials are parents now.** Millennials are growing up and with that come more responsibilities. Now one in four Millennials is already a parent, and that number is growing every day. As parents, Millennials are not changing their lifestyles to fit parenthood but are instead changing parenthood to fit their lifestyles. New generations of parents are raising their children in an economy fueled by economic hardships and digital innovation. Millennials, like the generations before them, are adapting to their new roles but are doing so in a way that is affecting brands on a global scale.

↻ **How can you help me?** Pragmatism is not just some philosophy Millennials were taught about in their high school history classes. They are living it. Pragmatism is rooted in the idea that success is based on how practical something is and how easily something can solve a problem. As parents, Millennials are paying more attention to brands that can make their lives easier. They are new to this parenting game but are changing the rules in terms of what wins and what does not win. Ultimately, useful has become the new cool and brands that adapt to that mind frame will see victory.

↻ **Millennial parents are not all the same.** As we can clearly see from a discussion of these orbits, Millennial parents are vastly different, not just from the general Millennial population but from each other as well. If we rely on stereotypes alone, Millennial parents would be self-centered, image conscious, and brand driven. We know this is not the case. Why? Parenthood changes people, and it changes people in different ways. Additionally, research from the Millennials as New Parents report shows that Millennial parents today hold less wealth than the Boomers and Gen Xers did at the same point in their lives. Diversity also plays a huge role when it comes to Millennial orbits. Millennials are giving birth to a new generation that will be, for the first time, a minority majority.

⊃ **The game is changing.** Millennials are a generation 80 million strong. They have the greatest influence over the way marketers are developing their strategic messages and campaigns. The traditional idea that a unique selling proposition will set your brand apart is no longer enough to draw in the pragmatic Millennial parent. Now brands must adapt to an environment where every brand is different. In order to stand apart they must develop a stronger brand story, recognize that technology is no longer new, and address Millennials as their primary consumers—they are no longer those jobless bums living at home.

CHAPTER 2

Welcome to the Ization Nation

What is it about the Millennial generation overall that really sets it apart from other generations? The desire to have unique experiences that are completely customized to each individual. This may not seem like a specifically Millennial trend, but extensive research shows that the Millennial generation is leading the way when it comes to colonizing the "Ization Nation." What is the Ization Nation, you ask? It is a new way of life that includes the *personalization*, *democratization*, and *casualization* of brand experiences. We all know that Millennials don't want to be told what to do; they want to be asked how to do it. Millennial parents especially, who are adjusting to their newfound authority in the home, want to share those new voices with the brands they are interacting with. Millennial par-

THE IZATION NATION ————
PERSONALIZATION
DEMOCRATIZATION
CASUALIZATION

ents are the most interactive group of consumers and expect brands to not just speak to them but actually listen to them. Brands that are embracing the Ization Nation and are offering Millennials premium-quality products at a low cost that are customized, personalized, and democratized will continue to win with Millennials.

Millennial parents don't want to just buy your brand; they want to be a part of it. They're looking for ways to participate, and they want to understand *why* you do what you do—otherwise known as your purpose, not just what you sell. In *Marketing to Millennials*, we wrote extensively about this participation economy, which in a nutshell means that consumers want to be your partners, not your target audience. Millennials expect to be a part of the process, cocreating products or services and the customer journey, and marketing with your organization.

As you can see, when it comes to Millennials and Millennial parents, cocreation is key, and, in fact, we have seen that both populations will pay a modest premium for a product if they are engaged with the brand. Although Millennial parents are more likely to make purchase decisions based on price, they are still willing to dish out the big bucks for products that have an impact on their family, such

MILLENNIALS WANT TO COCREATE ————
PRODUCTS & SERVICES
THE FULL CUSTOMER JOURNEY
MARKETING & COMMUNICATIONS

as auto and grocery purchases. (We will talk more about price vs. quality in Chapter 5.) As partners, Millennials across the board can actually help brands determine the best way to reach consumers through the concept of crowdsourcing, using social media, and other venues and techniques as vehicles for engagement and brand participation. This is true particularly for Millennial moms. According to Elizabeth Rizzo, senior vice president for reputation research at Weber Shandwick, "Marketers should appeal to Millennial moms' collaborative instincts. For example, Millennial moms are more likely than moms in general to share decision-making for groceries with someone else. This leaves the food and beverage industry open for a myriad of opportunities to create social platforms that connect Millennial moms to each other as well as other consumers for things like reviewing products, sharing deals/coupons, swapping recipes, etc." Platforms that allow moms to share their knowledge and connect with each other are ideal ways in which brands can appeal to the collaborative nature of Millennial moms and encourage them to be a part of the cocreation process.

We can see how this trend has reached full force when we think about the number of mommy blogs that have become increasingly popular in recent years. As a cohort, Millennial moms outblog college students (who are avid bloggers) 22 to 19 percent.[1] These blogs allow moms to share parenting advice, product recommendations, recipes, lifestyle suggestions, and more, with a community that they feel supports them. Research from the FutureCast "Mr. and Mrs. Millennial Mom and Dad" report shows that 71 percent of Millennial moms and dads rank parenting websites, online forums, parenting blogs, and social networks as their number one parental influence.[2] While connecting with their own parents is overwhelmingly the go-to for Millennials when it comes to questions regarding family care and advice, the fact that Millennial parents are so invested in their online communities shows that they value platforms that have a high level of participation.

In addition to participating, they want a reason to share your brand with their peer group, which is often achieved through disruption, authenticity, differentiation, or standing for a purpose that's more than your bottom line. (We'll get to Brand Stand in Chapter 3, so stand by.) Brands that have a purpose, brands that are radically transparent, brands that embrace conscious capitalism, brands that have disruptive schemas are inherently more shareworthy because at the root they aren't about the brand but about those who are sharing and how it makes them feel to share with their friends. This is how again and again, all of a sudden, a brand that has little or no budget comes out of nowhere and shakes things up. (We'll talk more about competitive forces in Chapter 3, too).

To better understand how important shareworthiness is, and how seemingly unknown brands can swoop in and become forces to be reckoned with, let's take a look at the innovative and widely popular Dollar Shave Club (DSC). It all started in 2011, when founders Michael Dubin and Mark Levine got fed up with spending $15 to $20 every time they bought new razor blades. After coming up with the idea to create a company that would sell razor blades for a cheaper price, they realized they could incorporate the convenience factor and take the hassle out of going to the store to buy new blades. Why not just deliver them straight to your front door? The model is simple: Register on the site and pay as little as $1 every month for the most basic but effective razor blade out there. Now, if you compare this upstart to the shave tech giants like Gillette and Schick, is it reasonable to think that DSC even stands a chance? Absolutely. Dollar Shave Club has what every brand is striving for right now: Millennial participation. According to the findings from a 2014 retail survey conducted by Forrester, 73 percent of Millennial men between the ages of 26 and 34 with at least one child under the age of 18 agree that they save time by shopping online. Additionally, 65 percent agree that they shop online because it is easier than going into a store.[3] Dollar Shave Club, unlike the traditional men's personal accessories and hygiene brands, realized the power of online engagement when connecting with Millennial men and those who are dads.

The company also strayed from traditional marketing tactics, favoring a more socially driven strategy instead. Dollar Shave Club released YouTube videos that went viral almost immediately, causing the social media world to take note and ask questions. Not to mention that those DSC videos are hilarious and appeal to the macho Millennial man who wants to save a few bucks and look good doing it. DSC's model completely disrupted the traditional practice of going to the store to buy razors and instead offered an innovation that reinvented the way men accomplish a daily task.

To enable you to visualize how to apply these theories, we created a handy-dandy participation/shareworthy matrix that can help organizations engage Millennials (see Figure 2–1).

The ideal is to have a brand that encourages a high level of Millennial participation and a high rate of sharing, as shown in the top right quadrant of the matrix in Figure 2–1. Chipotle has mastered the art of shareworthiness and reaps the benefits every day. Have

FIGURE 2–1   Participation/shareworthy matrix—old model.

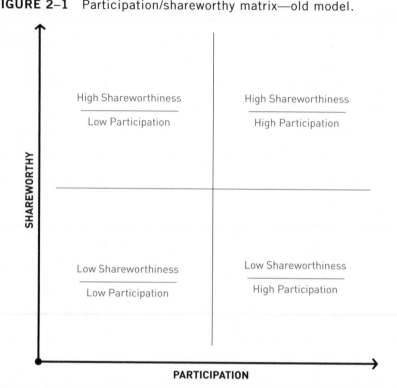

you ever been to Chipotle at lunchtime and not had to wait in line to get your burrito? Me either. Millennials are willing to pay the premium, in time and money, when it comes to a brand that has the same values as they do. Chipotle is known for its lack of traditional marketing, instead relying heavily on word-of-mouth promotion and longer videos that spread the message about the company's campaign, Cultivate a Better World. The videos "The Farmer" and "The Scarecrow" attack the processed-food industry and received a positive response from Millennial customers. The videos went viral almost instantly, each one garnering more than 8 million views since its creation. Viewers shared the video on their personal networks, and conversations were created within the digital space about Chipotle, its message, and its products.

This type of messaging strategy works well when connecting with Millennial parents. According to the 2014 Forrester Online Benchmark Survey, 37 percent of Millennial parents who engage with brands on social sites share interesting brand content with their family or friends. For Chipotle, that means these videos are being shared by one of the most vocal populations in our market. Not only does the company utilize the appropriate channels when connecting with Millennial parents, it also aligns with the health trends and local mentality strongly felt by Millennials in the 24-to-35 age group.[4]

Chipotle uses locally grown produce and organic meat and is one of the front-runners in educating consumers about the importance of eating better-quality ingredients, even at a fast-service casual-dining restaurant. The transparency, authenticity, and shareworthiness of the company combine to create a brand that Millennials not only enjoy but also believe in.

In addition to creating shareworthiness, Chipotle has also successfully encouraged consumer participation in its brand experience. Since 2011, Chipotle's Cultivate Food, Ideas & Music Festival has celebrated everyone who participates in Chipotle's ecosystem, including chefs, farmers, and consumers, all set to a hip soundtrack. Creating a brand experience and inviting consumers to not only be a part of it but get the inside scoop (yes, the company even shares the secret to its guacamole recipe) cultivates a sense of trust and partnership with the brand. Yelp reviewer Anthony M. felt the love: "I have a new respect for Chipotle. Chipotle cares about where its meat comes from. The animals have to be human[e]ly treated. In fact, they set up large posters you can read that compares what they do versus other restaurants. . . . Chipotle has no fear to share this information because they are doing it right. . . . Chipotle is an amazing company that understands what is good for its customers and the environment."[5]

This emphasis on participation aligns with how the definition of brand value has evolved over time. There was a time, just a few years back, when the formula for brand value looked something like this:

TRADITIONAL BRAND VALUE EQUATION

$$\text{BRAND VALUE} = \Sigma \ \frac{\text{Functional} + \text{Emotional Benefits}}{\text{Price}}$$

It's a simple formula: The benefits of a product, both emotional and functional, divided by price equate to value. For instance, if you make diapers that are bare-bottom design (some pun intended) with no bells and whistles, you're meeting a functional need but missing the mark in terms of emotional appeal. Therefore, the price of these diapers should be kept relatively low. If the diapers are made out of the finest materials and are specially engineered to reduce diaper rash and keep babies dry and comfortable, you are now meeting not only the functional needs of Mom and Dad but also their emotional needs by making them feel like good parents for keeping their precious one dry and happy. The cost of these diapers can be higher because of the value and emotional benefits they deliver.

With what we have learned about Millennials' desire to participate and share, we have updated the brand value equation like this:

MILLENNIAL FUELED BRAND VALUE EQUATION ⸺⸺⸺⸺⸺⸺⸺⸺⸺⸺⸺⸺⸺

$$\text{BRAND VALUE} = \sum \frac{\text{Functional} + \text{Emotional Benefits} + \textbf{PARTICIPATIVE BENEFITS}}{\textbf{TOTAL COST}}$$

The functional and emotional benefits are still key to inspiring
a premium price, but the benefits of consumer participation in the
brand are now incorporated into the equation. Let's go back to the
diaper example. Pampers is a premium diaper brand that provides a
quality product while tapping into the emotional benefits of being
a parent and taking the best care of your baby. When developing its
biggest innovation in the past twenty-five years, Pampers turned to
the experts—moms—to ensure that the company got it right. When
Cruisers with Dry Max were created, Pampers partnered with top
parenting organizations and panels of moms to test the diapers,
which received glowing results. Then consumers were encouraged
to go to Pampers.com to request free samples of these diapers (over
250,000 people did!), which was followed by a survey about their
experience. You can see how this process of including the consumer
in the brand experience creates a participative environment. All of
these components not only affect pricing but also create a brand
that is shareworthy. This sum is divided by the total cost. The total
cost of the product encompasses more than just the price, which
was the denominator in the old model. By dividing the sum of the
benefits by the total cost, we are taking time, convenience, and
the availability of the consumer into consideration in addition to the
actual price of the product.

Personalization

Let's go back to our participation/shareworthiness matrix for a moment. We'll be the first to admit that it is already time to update this model, which just goes to show the pace at which times are a-changin'. Organizations need to keep up. It's no surprise that the priorities of Millennials shift once they have children. A recent BabyCenter survey showed that, before kids, the priorities of Millennial moms were, in this order: romance, fashion, me time, and fitness. After kids, their number one priority, not surprisingly, was the well-being of their children, with the priority level of all those former activities dropping significantly.[6] Additionally, time and money are often at a premium for the Millennial parent. This trend is not Millennial-specific, but the way a contemporary mom interacts with her children is completely different from the way mothers in previous generations did. Her desire for products that were uniquely for her is now transitioning into a desire for products that are completely unique for her child. The higher value placed on time means that new moms are more interested in creating experiences for their children and families that are worthwhile and a good use of their time. This is where the importance of personalization comes in. Millennial parents are creating a parenting style that is completely different from that of previous generations, focusing on the uniqueness each parent brings to the family. The same BabyCenter report found that the Millennial mom describes her parenting style as more relaxed, fun, forgiving, and aspirational than her Gen X mom counterpart.[7]

When we think about Millennial parents, it is important to realize that they do not approach parenting the same way as Generation X and Boomer parents—especially when it comes to household structure. Traditionally, the household functioned in a very top-down way. Laurie Klein, senior vice president of The Family Room, LLC, explains "The traditional family consisted of two parents and approximately two kids. The role of a parent in past generations was to be the authority figure, the disciplinarian and the coach. It was a parent's job to lay out the game plan, explain it to a child and ask them to go and execute the plan. Today, the 'traditional family' is in the minority. A family today can consist of a single parent household, a same sex couple household, a multigenerational household, a traditional husband/wife household, or a blended family as the husband/wife and kids from a previous marriage come together. Basically, we define a family as anyone living under the same roof. What's even more surprising is how the relationship has shifted today between parents and kids. Although today's millennial parents are still the final authority, they are more likely to say that their child is a friend. These millennial parents are also likely to describe their role as a mentor and their relationship with their child as very collaborative. Instead of acting as a coach with a game plan, today's parents are the cheerleaders for their children." According to research conducted by The Family Room, when parents were asked whether or not they considered their child to be a best friend, 60 percent of Millennial parents today said that they "agreed/completely agreed" that their child was their best friend, which is an increase over previous generations. Additionally, this research revealed that Millennial parents are more likely to say that their children are less fearful of them than they were of their own parents when they were growing up.

Marketers have always considered two specific strategies for getting a foot in the door with families: (1) Target the parent when the product has benefits that are most relevant to the adult or (2) target the kids when it is something that kids are passionate about (such as presweetened cereals, fruit snacks, or toys). However, The Family Dynamix Study from The Family Room found that there are five different decision-making typologies that families use most frequently today: Because I Said So, Board of Directors, Family Meeting, Parent Screen, and Kids Cut Loose. Surprisingly, when asked about a wide range of decisions that families had recently made, the large majority of decisions had been made using a collaborative decision-making style such as Board of Directors, Family Meeting, or Parent Screen. It was much less likely that parents were making the decision on their own (Because I Said So) or that kids were calling the shots (Kids Cut Loose). In fact, collaborative decision-making styles were used almost twice as frequently among Millennial families vs. parents or kids making decisions solely on their own. Klein says, "When considering how to appeal to Millennial families today, it's important to understand the entire family perspective about your brand, since it's likely that all family members will have input into the brand decision." The most successful brands are now featuring full families in their advertisements rather than just a few members or just the parents.

Cheerios does an excellent job of portraying the family holistically rather than targeting just one member. In a 2014 Super Bowl commercial, Cheerios features two Millennial parents telling their daughter that she is going to have a baby brother by counting the Cheerios laid out on the table. Not only is the family multicultural (a true reflection of many Millennial families today), but the commercial also approaches the Millennial family dynamic in a realistic and relatable way. After a moment of quiet contemplation, the daughter responds by adding another Cheerio to the pile, saying a dog will be a new addition to the family as well. Mom and Dad share a look before Dad agrees. While this is a subtle take on the family decision making of Millennial parents, the ad was extremely effective because it portrayed a real situation and adapted it to a very modern and very personal moment for a Millennial family.

Therefore, in our new model, participation and shareworthiness are still components of brand value, but we've added one more element: *personalization*. (See Figure 2–2.)

While participation is the consumers' ability to partner in the creation of your brand or product, personalization is the consumers' ability to customize your brand, product, or experience in a way that is unique to them. It is no surprise that personalization can pro-

FIGURE 2–2 Personalization Venn diagram—new model.

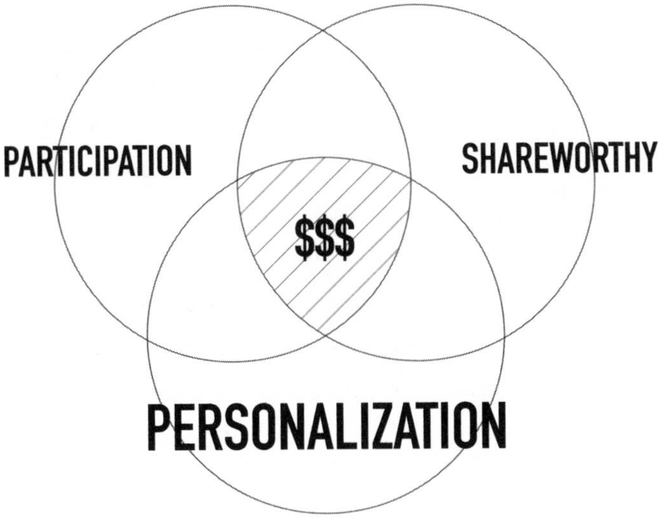

vide a winning point of differentiation for many brands engaging the Millennial audience. For example, when Millennials approach the fashion industry, many are looking for a product that enhances their own personal style—not one that makes them conform to what everyone else is wearing. Millennials care more about how a brand can fit their image than how they can fit into the brand's image. This is especially true for young parents who feel as though their identity has changed since they became a mom or dad. According to a lifestyle study conducted by ad agency DDB, 25 percent of Millennial dads say they have lost their sense of identity since becoming a father. Personalization and customization allow these young men to redefine who they are in their new role and feel more confident knowing there is something that makes them unique.[8] Denise Delahorne of DDB shares, "You traditionally bought a tie [for Dad] because it was generic, functional and you didn't know what else to get him. But millennial dads are interested in the latest clothes and fashion."[9] Ultimately, Millennials desire products that are unique and can be customized to fit their specific needs. If a product is perceived as unique, it is more likely that a Millennial will connect with the brand. Millennial shoppers value differentiation when looking for new products and will go out of their way to find something that no one else has. According to FutureCast's research on Millennials, almost 55 percent of female Millennials who participated in the study have a unique item that won't be seen on everyone else.[10]

This desire for differentiation and personalization also drives Millennial parents when they make purchasing decisions. Brands connecting with Millennial parents must walk a thin line between portraying the traditional family setting (mom at home and dad at work) and the new modern family model—one that may include a single mother, a stay-at-home dad, or same-sex parents. Creating dynamic messages for different family types allows every type of parent to be reached and provides more opportunities for engagement and conversation. For example, Image First parents crave personalization to bolster their own personal image. However, positioning personalization as a way to stand out among your peers will not resonate with a parent in the Family First orbit. Moms and dads in the Family First orbit are more likely to respond positively to messages that allow them to create a personalized experience for their family. For example, a stroller brand may target Image First parents by explaining all of the new high-tech features of the stroller. The advertisement might show very fit, trendy parents running with their child in the stroller while all of the other parents at the park watch in awe and with a hint of envy. The Family First targeted advertisement, however, might show a family going to the park together and Mom storing everything she needs in the stroller—there is ample room for a baby bag, her purse, and snacks. In both scenarios the stroller is the featured product, but in the shift from bolstering a personal image of the parent to enhancing the image of the family is where we see the difference in messaging personalization for these two orbits.

In many ways, the integration of technology into our lives has also driven the concept and ability to personalize at the individual consumer level. And this integration goes beyond just the Millennial mom and dad. Have you ever seen a two-year-old navigate an iPad better than you? Have you witnessed a toddler desperately trying to navigate a laptop by touching and swiping the screen (with sticky fingers)? It is no surprise that the children of Millennials are not only interested in the technology that Mom and Dad use but seem to intuitively understand how to use it.

As a result, success can also be found in personalized technology solutions for children that tap into the parents' desire to educate and entertain, without the side dish of guilt. One company that has successfully created a niche in this space is StoryBots, created by the brothers who founded JibJab Media (best known for "insert your face" viral political and holiday cartoons). After becoming parents themselves, they watched their own children seamlessly engage in technology and saw an opportunity. They also saw an opportunity to create educational entertainment for children that would not drive parents crazy. Do Millennials even have the constitution to sit through the endless repetition of Barney the Dinosaur's "I love you, you love me" song? Are you singing it in your head just from reading that last sentence? Sorry about that.

Like a virtual *Sesame Street*, StoryBots has created a world of unique creatures that, through multiple platforms, provide personalized educational entertainment for children. The StoryBots experience can be personalized for the child through the Starring You® books and videos, which leverage the technology created by JibJab to add your child's picture to animated storybooks and music videos. Educational videos feature lessons about the ABCs, music, and animals using catchy tunes designed not to drive parents crazy. In fact, their website boasts that StoryBots provides "sanity-saving tools" for parents, acknowledging that it's not always fun for parents to engage in the programming their children find entertaining. They even won the National Parenting Center Seal of Approval in 2013.

The winning combo for StoryBots is product personalization, appeal to parents as well as children, and offering a guilt-free solution to handing off the ol' iPad or smartphone to your kids. The mommy blogger behind Artchoo.com, Jeanette Nyberg, says,

"When I finally opened it, lying in bed with Beckett, we were both instantly smitten. It's smart, amazingly illustrated and animated, and the songs are reminiscent of They Might Be Giants, and rival the catchiest pop songs, but are absolutely not annoying."[11] Brands that want to connect with Millennial parents in a way that allows them to personalize experiences, technology, and messaging should be taking notes from this relatively young company that is winning with new parents.

Another company that appreciates the need for personalization is IKEA. In 1985, IKEA opened its first store in the United States. The flat-pack model (which you may know as do-it-yourself assembly with that little Allen wrench) allows IKEA to keep its products affordable by reducing transportation expenses, lowering storage space requirements, decreasing damage during transport, and reducing labor costs. For consumers, it means simple, stylish, functional furniture at great prices. Many Millennials who are new parents are also first-time homeowners. This means that instead of worrying about what outfit to buy for their next party, they are deciding what crib to buy for the nursery. IKEA has created a brand that is extremely pragmatic and gives Millennial parents the opportunity to purchase relatively high-quality home products for a much lower cost than other options in the market today. IKEA has been by their side from dorm to apartment to first family home.

IKEA has long appealed to a younger audience, offering furniture and organizational solutions for small spaces like dorm rooms and compact apartments. Mike Ward, IKEA USA president, acknowledges that perception but notes that the growth areas of the company are expanding beyond them. "Traditionally, people think we are good for college students and storage. What we find is that our growth is coming from the main areas of the home like the living room, kitchen, and bedroom."[12]

However, as customers get older, there is a loss of brand affinity among the more casual IKEA shoppers as they transition to more aspirational furniture brands like Ethan Allen, Crate and Barrel, and Pottery Barn. Mary Lunghi, IKEA's strategic insights manager for the United States, says, "We've identified that we have a leaky bucket and that our strongest most loyal base is the under 34 set. They have the highest awareness, highest consideration, and sharpest affinity for the brand." This leaky bucket has caused IKEA to ask why it is losing out on customers as they age and how it can prevent that from happening in the future, particularly with Millennials.

IKEA came to the conclusion that, while the functionality and affordability of its furniture appeal to Millennials, the mass-produced furniture is not allowing them to truly express themselves and share their feelings, ideas, and uniqueness with the world. How can they do that with a matching white desk, bookcase, and chair? Lunghi comments, "The key issue is that they want to be able to know that they can personalize and individualize our products to be able to show their creativity and their need to curate. Currently, we do well with younger customers from a functional perspective, but in order for the relationship to continue, they definitely need to be able to build on the functional foundation by being able to add their individuality and constantly curate."

IKEA leveraged these insights to fuel its innovative social media campaign. It wasn't that IKEA needed to change the furniture to offer more colors or customization; it just needed to invite Millennials to participate in the brand. As we know, Millennials want to cocreate the brand, journey, and marketing, and they want a reason to share it with their network. This situation is no different with Millennial parents. With this in mind, IKEA created Share Space, which is a website designed to engage customers in sharing the unique ways that they customize their furniture. The Share Space website explains, "The IKEA Share Space is made by everyday people. You don't have to be an interior designer, just a lover of design. It's a place where you can admire rooms you like and save them. You can even select IKEA products to save to your wish list."[13] For first-time parents who have never added a nursery to their home and are not quite sure where to start, Share Space creates a starting point. It enables them to collect ideas from their peers and create their own personalized nursery with IKEA products using the different tools provided in the platform.

Personalization does not just apply to branded products but to services as well. For Millennial parents, the desire to personalize often happens before the baby is even born. Shawnee Mission Medical Center, located in the Kansas City area, has long been a leader in caring for women and babies. When the hospital faced the decision of whether to renovate the existing birthing center or create a new one from scratch, Millennial moms played a large role. Doug Spear, administrative director for marketing and strategic development for the hospital, said, "As the millennials have come on board, we've noticed that their tastes have changed, how they access healthcare has changed and what prompts them to access certain healthcare has changed."

One major difference is Millennial moms' propensity to shop around for the hospital at which they will give birth. It used to be that your doctor practiced at only one hospital, he or she made the referral for the prospective mother, and she gave birth there. End of story. Now, with doctors often practicing at multiple hospitals and consumers accustomed to having more choices and information, the decision is often much more consumer focused. "Millennials take more shopping tours," says Spear, "where potential patients get a tour of the birth center. From an aesthetics standpoint, on the front end, they are much more concerned about the look of the hospital and the nurses." Millennials are generally looking for a hospital experience that is less, well, hospital-y or sterile-looking and instead, want more of a hotel or even home environment. The new birthing center, which uses dark wood, more natural light, and backlit mirrors, was created with this in mind.

Shawnee Mission Medical Center also had to consider the issue of technology and the role it plays in the birthing process. Spear explains, "Technology at the birthing center used to be viewed as intrusive, but now it is the status quo. The moment the baby is born, the world knows it." Most Millennial moms and dads bring technology, including iPads, smartphones, and laptops, with them to share the event with friends and family. Instead of fighting it, the new birthing center integrated and embraced technology to provide new mothers with a birthing experience that they can share. The hospital has also worked to incorporate the convenience of technology into the new model. Parents who bring their own devices can order meals online, and those who don't can use the interactive TVs in each room to log onto social media and order meals. The hospital is working toward a "room service" model to provide even more instant gratification to new moms and dads.

Personalization is the driving force behind the Ization Nation. Though there are many components to this new way of life, the personalization of any brand experience is what truly connects with

Millennials and makes them want to interact with a brand. Maintaining a strong sense of self-identity is incredibly important to Millennial parents. As these young adults are taking on more responsibility, they still expect brands to enhance their own sense of self through personalized and customizable experiences. Millennial moms specifically have thirteen hours less time to themselves in an average month than they did before they became mothers, so brands that embrace their motherhood while also strengthening each mother's own self-identity will see positive feedback. Millennial parents, as we know, are also putting their own spin on parenting and desire brands that allow them to also put that personal spin on the products they are purchasing. Millennials grew up watching marketers homogenize their parents' generation, and they do not want that to happen again. The push for personalization is the Millennial parents' resistance to losing their self-identity. Anything that allows them to feel unique and one-of-a-kind and can enhance the quality of family life is a win for the Millennial parent.

Democratization

Remember the time when information wasn't easily available at the click of a button or the swipe of your thumb? Millennials don't. Millennials have grown up in an age in which the concept of democracy doesn't apply just to our government. Now everything has been democratized, so that consumers have a say in almost all aspects of the nation's economy. Think of this new ideology as the "democratization of everything." Despite the fact that they have lived through times of great economic stress, Millennials have been able to see and experience far more of the world than any generation before.

Millennials began this movement long before they were parents, but now that they have taken on these new roles and are supporting more than just themselves, they are expecting products, advice, information, and the like, to be readily available at a moment's notice. Does this affect how brands market to Millennials, you ask? It sure does. Brands no longer have ownership of their image; consumers are now primary stakeholders of a brand's image.

Does this concept sound familiar? Recall Abraham Lincoln and his famous Gettysburg Address. One of the guiding principles of our nation, as stated by Lincoln, is that it is a country "of the people, by the people, for the people." In this same way, brands are no longer a monarchy that rules over consumers. Instead, they are partners and are expected to not only act with the best interest of all consumers in mind but to do so with the understanding that consumers have the ability to push out and generate content outside of the brand's control. This revolution came about as social media became mainstream and, dare we say, normal. It brought sweeping changes to our social and political landscape, and the people who were first born into (and in some cases invented) it are now moms and dads.

Kickstarter, an online crowdfunding platform, dramatically changed the way people raise money, make donations, and support the creative communities they choose to be a part of. Founded entirely on the idea of connectivity, Kickstarter has created an environment that not only emphasizes the democratization of everything but also encourages users to openly share their ideas with their peers around the world. Since the site was initiated five years ago, 6.8 million people have pledged $1 billion, funding 66,000 creative projects. Projects on Kickstarter range from book publications to movie productions to one young gentleman who raised $55,492 in order to make homemade potato salad (no, we did not make this one up).

One of the most successful Kickstarter campaigns was the recent Reading Rainbow campaign that raised more than $5 million in an effort to bring a library of interactive books and platforms to classrooms in need. If you are a Baby Boomer or Gen Xer, there is a good chance that you know LeVar Burton as Geordi La Forge from *Star Trek*. However, to a Millennial, LeVar Burton is the man with the soothing voice who hosted *Reading Rainbow*, which aired on PBS from 1983 to 2006. In an effort to bring awareness to issues affecting classroom literacy, Burton turned to Kickstarter to create a fund-raising campaign that reached out to sentimental Millennial parents who remembered *Reading Rainbow* from their childhood. Many Millennial parents have now reached the dreaded 3-0 and are just old enough to begin feeling nostalgic about their childhoods. According to research conducted by Kate Loveland, a Ph.D. candidate at Arizona State University, large milestones, such as starting a family or turning 30, trigger an emotional desire to feel connected to a larger group. Many individuals, specifically Millennials, regress to products from their childhood that typically remind them of a simpler time. Now that Millenials have children of their own, Loveland asserts, they can "create a symbolic, shared experience between the mom and the child."[14] What could be more special than sharing story time with your little ones?

The money raised from this campaign will be used to expand the Reading Rainbow app, which was previously offered only on the iPad and Kindle Fire. When asked why they focused on expanding the app rather than bringing the show back to daytime television, Burton responded, "When we launched *Reading Rainbow*, TV was the prevailing tech of the day to reach kids. [However,] kids today use TV as just one screen, so if you want to reach them you have to be on all of them."[15] Why do you think children are so digitally focused? Their parents are the original digital natives.

The Reading Rainbow Kickstarter campaign is a prime example of democratization in action because it applies all the principles of a successful democratized marketing plan. The campaign reached consumers on a variety of different platforms focusing predominantly on social media—the most democratized outlet. Millennial parents who had strong connections to *Reading Rainbow* not only made donations themselves but also shared the page and essentially partnered with the company in its efforts to spread awareness. In other words, the ownership of the campaign was transferred from the brand to the people—a key element in the democratization of the brand experience. As we can see from this example, democratization is transforming the roles of key stakeholders. Figure 2–3 displays these changes in a table format. As we can see, the language used to describe the roles of each key stakeholder (consumers, brands, and marketers) has become much more inclusive, meaning that the most successful brands have transitioned from an era of the "con"sumer to one of the "pro"sumer. The "pro"sumer is someone who takes ownership over his or her own marketing and expects a more leveled playing field in regard to brand access.

The process of democratization relies on the fact that what was once available only for a few is now available for, and can be controlled by, the general public. In the true spirit of democracy, many brands are adjusting the way they do business in order to provide "luxury" services or products to all consumers. This will ultimately

FIGURE 2–3   Democratization of key stakeholders.

STAKEHOLDERS	OLD MODEL	NEW MODEL
CONSUMERS	Reactive	Proactive
	Passive	Aggressive
	Predictable	Insight-driven
	Target Audience	Brand Partner
	"Con"sumer	"Pro"sumer
BRANDS	Idea / Content Curator	Encourage user-generated content
	Profit-oriented	Engagement-oriented
	Exclusive	Inclusive
	Creator	Cocreators
	Static	Flexible
MARKETING	Mass Messaging	Brand Stand
	Brand Controlled	User Controlled
	Traditional Advertising	Social Media and Content Advertising
	One-Way	Two-Way
	Short-term	Long-term

lead to a democratization of technology across all platforms. As an example, think about tech in the automotive space. Just five years ago, Bluetooth and voice recognition systems were available only in select cars and were considered luxury accessories. Now they are standard systems and, in some states, are even required by law to be included in the automotive software. Millennial parents are looking for cars that have the capability to protect their most precious cargo. Brands that can offer that protection through innovation and technology will see a higher number of Millennial parents at their dealerships. Ford has adapted to this changing environment by offering the same technology in all car models, not just the top-of-line options.

Ford was one of the first automotive brands to introduce high-quality technology systems across its model line instead of starting with high-end cars and letting the technology trickle down through the manufacturer's vehicle lineup. The Microsoft Sync system is a new platform that combines infotainment with navigation systems and enables hands-free calling and safety assist features. When it was first released in 2012, the launch was concentrated largely on the Focus—an economy car that is more popular with Millennial car buyers on a budget—typically those young adults who were starting families. Ford is not the only brand transitioning into this democratized model of production. In order to connect with Millennial consumers, companies are realizing that they must work for the people and by the people instead of the traditional model that divided consumers based on income level and other exclusive factors.

Take a minute to think about which market is the most income-sensitive. Got it? Are you thinking it's the housing market? If you are, you are correct. It can be argued that the housing market is one of the most divided markets in the United States. U.S. Commerce Department and Labor Department data for the 100 largest metropolitan areas by population shows that the disparity between the tenth most expensive region and the ninetieth most expensive region by home prices is at the widest it has been since record keeping began in 1969.[16] Millennials who are new parents and are living on a budget have been greatly affected by the housing market because the crash occurred when many young adults were stepping into parenthood for the first time. A large portion of the Millennial population is putting off buying a house and is instead turning to rental options. According to a survey conducted by Zillow, an online real estate marketplace, 100 economists nationwide expect home-ownership rates in the next five years to be lower than the current rates of 64.7 percent.[17] However, Millennials will have enormous influence in the coming years as they begin to get married and start families—two of the biggest reasons for first-time home purchases. Survey results from Coldwell Banker Real Estate found that 79 percent of Millennial parents make major purchase decisions based on their children.[18] This means that brands in the housing sector must approach Millennial parents differently, as they are acting in a different way and with different intentions than what we have seen in the past.

Ultimately, home purchasing is another example of how the family decision-making model has shifted as a result of new Millennial parent behaviors and mindsets. This has also led to a greater democratization of the real estate industry. With more people involved in the decision, easy access to more information when considering a home purchase is required to satisfy today's consumer. Millennial parents want more information, more access to resources, and more personalized help in making their decisions. These needs (or desires) go beyond the traditional information required to make a home purchase such as square footage, number of bedrooms, and lot size.

Zillow recognized the changing homebuyers' needs and created an online platform that allows users to connect with each other and ultimately be in charge of their own real estate endeavors. The website boasts: "We are transforming the way consumers make home related decisions and connect with professionals." This platform screams democracy. Additionally, to appease parents who include their children (or their children's needs) in their purchase decision, detailed neighborhood and school information is provided, including school ratings and distance from schools to home, not to mention a popularity rating to ensure that home shoppers are selecting homes that others are interested in, too.

Traditionally, working with a real estate agent was costly and time consuming, but Zillow is creating a space where Millennial parents do not have to be wealthy to access information. According to Crystal Webster, a premier real estate agent from Kansas City, "Most of the millennial parents I work with have already looked online before they come to me. Zillow gives them an idea of what they are going to get for their price points and determine the areas they want to live." Ultimately, online sites like Zillow create a starting point for new homebuyers. However, that does not mean Millennial parents are shying away from working face-to-face with a real estate agent because they still crave that personal connection. Webster explains that young parents typically start looking online for a new home eighteen months before they are ready to buy and will meet with an agent six months before they make a purchase. The combination of online crowdsourcing and traditional real estate agents has fueled a democratized housing market where Millennials are more empowered than any other generation and have access to resources and networks that were considered exclusive in previous generations.

Democracy is no longer just a political ideology. It has now expanded into the marketing industry in a trend that is entirely Millennial-fueled. Millennial parents, especially, believe in the freedom to access information and products from any platform. They want everything to be equal and fair, and they will reward brands that participate in this Democracy of Fairness. In an ode to our forefathers who fought for our American freedoms, "long live democracy" . . . of everything!

Casualization

The trend of casualization is not a new one, and by no means does it belong to Millennials alone. Millennials weren't even a twinkle in their parents' eyes when women's bathing suits evolved into the bikini from what looked like a conservative onesie. There were no Millennials when people stopped dressing up to go to the airport, a restaurant, or church. Over time, we have witnessed a loosening of formalities such as registering for a dinnerware pattern when getting married and sending thank-you notes. Millennials, however, have certainly taken the casualization torch and run with it. Even the process of sharing photos and memories is no longer about passing down but about passing around.

Instagram and Facebook have been among the largest contributors to this new trend. Baby books are no longer hardbound photo albums. Instead, they are online digital albums that include videos, Animotos (video or photo slide shows quickly created with existing pictures), messages, voice recordings, and personalized images. When Mom and Dad see their one-year-old taking his or her first steps, they are not busting out their video recorder, they are using their iPhone to record that special moment and instantly post it to Facebook. In ten years, when the children of Millennial parents start dating, there will be no pulling the album off the shelf and dusting off the cover to share the bare-bottom bath-time pictures.

Now those memories and images are just a simple click (or swipe) away. Let's revisit our Millennial parent orbits to better understand this transformation and casualization of the baby book. Remember the Style and Substance orbit? These are Millennial parents who are very socially driven and use their social media profiles to expand both their family and their personal networks. Facebook is the most appropriate place for these parents to post pictures of their family because they view their profile as a hub for sharing photos and videos. This transformation from a more formal and traditional way of capturing moments to a more casual, socially driven way is one that will continue to influence young parents as Millennials start their own families.

Another area where Millennials have had a strong influence is in the casualization of language. The new currency is time, which means that marketing messages must be more concise and to the point. Now almost every message must fit within 140 characters or less (thanks to Twitter). This has led to an era of abbreves (translation: abbreviations) and slang terms that have not only shortened words but have also shortened the way in which they are communicated. While these shorthand phrases are not specific to the Millennial parent population, they do resonate with overall generational trends that are influenced by the entire Millennial population. The popular Millennial Parents YouTube series, which features short videos on life as Millennial parents, is filled with colloquial language that Millennials and Millennial parents use every day. If you have not yet watched these videos, we highly recommend them—they hit the nail on the head when it comes to personifying the average Millennial parent. Let's examine two of the most popular Millennial shorthand words introduced during the past year:

YOLO—The acronym for the phrase "you only live once" became widely popular after the Drake song "The Motto" was in-

YOLO

"You should eat that cookie. YOLO."
"Let's go out tonight! YOLO!"
"Grab your GoPro, let's skydive. YOLO, right?"

troduced in 2013. Millennials swarmed to the phrase, using it for almost every possible situation.

Chillax—The way "radical" described the 1980s, "chill" describes the Millennials who grew up with California rock permeating the airwaves. "Chill" is the casual way of responding to just about anything. But, wait, there's more! Millennials have taken it one step further by creating the word "chillax." A combination of "chill" and "relax," "chillax" is one of the few words that can act as a noun, an adjective, and a verb. "Chillax" has led to a casualization when it comes to describing a person or situation.

These are only two examples of an entire language developed by the Millennial generation. When marketers are connecting with Millennial parents, those in the Image First and Against the Grain orbits would be the most responsive to this type of communication. They are highly connected via their mobile devices and are the

CHILLAX

"How's your day going so far?" "Oh, you know, it's pretty chillax."
"Do you want to hang out later?" "Yeah, let's just grab a movie and chillax."
"What are you up to today?" "Nothing really, just chillaxing."

most likely to engage in conversation with brands on their social networks. Against the Grain parents specifically like to follow their favorite brands on social networks and often participate in an online dialogue. For brands that connect with these Millennials, doing so in their "own language" is a key engagement tactic that can lead to positive outcomes.

In 2010, Toyota created a campaign that reinvented the minivan. Even from the early days when the Dodge Caravan first rolled off the assembly line, the car was designed for the rushed soccer mom who did not have time to worry about outward appearances. For decades, the minivan has been a symbol of conformity that represents the inevitable move to the "burbs" after starting a family. Like the generations before them, Millennial parents were less keen on switching to a minivan because of the connotations that were associated with the "mom van." Millennials viewed minivans as clunky, too big, inefficient gas-guzzlers that just didn't align with how they viewed themselves. In order to reinvent the minivan image, Toyota embraced the Millennial mentality and created the Swagger Wagon. The campaign featured the typical Millennial family rapping about their car, their family, and, most important, their swagger. Essentially, swagger is the way you present yourself to others and the world around you. The way you handle situations is an indication of your swagger level. Swagger is shown from how the person handles a situation." Having swagger is typically associated with confidence, pride, and all-around awesomeness. (Listen to the song "Swagga Like Us," by Jay-Z, T.I., Kanye West, and Lil Wayne, for the full lowdown on swagger.) The Swagger Wagon (because how dare it be referred to as a minivan?) is an ode to all those families who own a Sienna SE for the space but fill it with family swagger.

The YouTube music video for the campaign garnered more than 12 million views, and Millennial parents were more on board with the idea of a van than ever. As a result of the massive digital effort, the Sienna YouTube channel was one of the most watched stations for weeks, and the videos trended on both Twitter and Facebook. However, what really made this ad such a success was not the catchiness of the song (even though you won't be able to get it out of your head for days); it was the fact that Millennials got it. Toyota spoke to Millennials in their own language. The message of the campaign wasn't "Buy this car because you can fit everything you will ever need in it." Instead, the focus was on embracing who you are as a parent and the irony of being "cool" while driving a minivan. What parent doesn't want to be considered cool?

Another common practice that emphasizes the casualization within the Millennial generation is taking a "selfie." What started as a generational trend took hold in the greater population and now everyone, from President Obama to Ellen DeGeneres, is constantly posting selfies online.

> **Selfie**—Who would have thought that the forward-facing camera on a smartphone would lead to a revolution known today as the "selfie"? The creation of Snapchat and other applications that encourage users to take selfies is a phenomenon that does not seem to be slowing down. Even Ellen DeGeneres jumped on board when she hosted the 2014 Academy Awards and took the most shared selfie of all time with some of the biggest names in Hollywood (and Lupita Nyong'o's brother). A new Pew Research Center study found that 55 percent of all Millennial participants had

posted a selfie to a social media site.[19] Although Millennials may not be the selfish generation they were once thought to be, they certainly are the "selfie generation."

Which brand took the selfie to a whole new level? GoPro. Founder Nick Woodman created the portable, handheld, life-proof camera in 2004 when he wanted to find a way to capture his epic surfing moments to share with his friends. The GoPro "point-of-view" footage has ramped up the selfie trend by 100 watts. Now young consumers are not just taking pictures of themselves but are instead taking video of themselves and, more important, of what they see, creating a casualization of self-documentary.

This technology offers completely authentic footage from any crazy adventure or life-changing situation. The invention of the GoPro opened the door for brands to create raw stories as told from the perspective of their customers. As user-generated content is becoming more mainstream in marketing campaigns, GoPro technology is in demand for brands across the market. When it comes to creating content, all the company has to do is hand out cameras and watch the magic happen.

GoPro is also reinventing the way families capture those magical moments. Woodman told *Forbes* magazine that he had a camera strapped to his chest during the delivery of his sons.[20] This type of videography creates a whole new genre that Woodman refers to as "life moments." This brings the GoPro from the adventure space into the family home and allows new families to integrate the highest-quality technology into their daily lives. The mission of GoPro is to "help people capture their meaningful experiences with others—and celebrate them together."[21] Isn't that what every parent wants to do? In the future, we can imagine that GoPro will not be used exclusively for extreme sports footage but will be the go-to camera for families and communities who want to share experiences and create memories together.

However, the most well-known and influential Millennial addition and casualization of language has been the hashtag. Hashtags have become more than just a way to communicate—they are now starting trends that create conversations and key touch points. Brands that adapt to trends like #tbt (throw back Thursday), #mancrushmonday, #womancrushwednesday, to name a few, are instantly winning with Millennials because they are speaking the Millennial language. Many industry professionals have also argued that the hashtag is becoming the URL of the Millennial generation, and they would not be far off base with this assumption. Twitter was the first social media giant to utilize the hashtag in 2007, and since then almost every other outlet uses hashtags to track conversation, generate and guide traffic, and organize trends.

General Mills recently introduced its new campaign for Peanut Butter Cheerios, which was a huge win with the Millennial parent demographic. The campaign featured a two-minute portrayal of how Dad makes mornings awesome by serving Peanut Butter Cheerios. What is so great about the advertisement is that the focus is not on the product; instead, it is about something deeper than that: how to be a good dad. In fact, the tagline for the entire campaign is #HowtoDad—no mention of the product at all. Since July 20, 2014, when the spot first aired on YouTube, there have been more than 1 million total views. Many Millennial parents jumped on board, tweeting their support for and positive feedback on the advertisement on their personal pages. One user tweeted, "Thank you, Cheerios, for making a commercial that celebrates fathers rather than making them look foolish. #howtodad." The use of a hashtag as a campaign slogan generated quite a bit of online buzz and emphasizes how impactful the Millennial casualization of language is becoming. The hashtag was ultimately the only call to action for consumers in the entire two-minute video, emphasizing the importance of generating conversation and brand love before expecting sales and loyalty. In the future, agencies may begin to incorporate a "hashtag marketer," who would be responsible for following online trends and creating real-time conversations with brand partners. As the casualization of language is becoming even more prevalent, brands that are addressing Millennials and Millennial parents in their own language will have a better chance of seeing a response than those that don't.

So how can companies with a formal or traditional background appeal to these uber-casual Millennials? Jeanette Carter, vice president of integrated consumer marketing at Hallmark, believes that leaning into this casualization, not fighting it, is the answer. "It's about relating to the millennial perspective, being relevant to their life," she says. "You cannot 'build it and they will come.' You have to lean into what they are already doing."

How does Hallmark change its voice to appeal to the Millennial parent customer without alienating its core customer? By recognizing the similarities between customer types (they want to connect with the people they care about) as well as the differences (they are confident and want to do it in their own voice). And that's exactly what Hallmark is doing with its latest line of greeting cards, Studio Ink, specifically targeted to Millennials. "You have to keep things new and fresh," says Carter, "create smaller customer segments so you can deliver more relatable content." This new line of cards is geared to those looking for an authentic and unexpected way to connect with other Millennials. Each card is open-ended to allow for a more personal card-giving experience. Young, up-and-coming artists and writers create the cards. Though not specifically targeting Millennial parents, the Studio Ink line allows parents and nonparents to connect in a new way.

Casualization, like every other "Ization" in the Ization Nation, is a key element in the new strategies brands must implement in order to win over the most powerful demographic to date. Even the workplace is completely restructuring itself to align with the more casual Millennial generation. Many corporate offices are now offering more flexibility in working hours. Millennial parents especially expect more support from their employers when it comes to work/life balance. Although many Millennials are breaking away from tradition, there is still a strong belief among the Millennial parent population that it is important for at least one parent to stay home with their children during the early years. According to the findings from the FutureCast and Vision Critical Millennial Parent survey, 60 percent of Millennial parents say that their preschoolers are cared for at home. The data does not explicitly say who is taking care of the children while they are home, but it can be assumed that either one parent is staying home, in-laws are helping, or a full-time sitter/nanny is employed. However, Millennial parents still want to be involved in their children's lives and feel more comfortable when both parents can be available for child care. Therefore, Millennials are placing higher value on companies that allow them to create a stable work/life balance. According to research conducted by the Working Mother Institute, the Millennial generation feels freer than any other generation to choose between work and staying home. Unlike older generations, working Millennial parents agree they like to compartmentalize work and family time. For Millennial parents who are also employees, the ability to separate work life from home life allows them to be more focused on the tasks at hand—whether that means focusing all of their attention on bedtime stories in the evening or writing reports in the afternoon. In contrast, Baby Boomer and Generation X employees feel a need to be "always working" and appreciate that technology allows them to work from home at night and on the weekends.[22] This casualization of the workplace goes beyond just the transition from suits and ties to polo shirts and jeans; it is a complete shift in the way the office is run to accommodate this more relaxed and balanced generation.

CHAPTER 2: KEY TAKEAWAYS

⊃ **The model is changing ... again.** Previously, brand value was determined by the emotional and functional benefits of a product divided by the price. Now the ante has been upped, and participative benefits and shareability are part of the equation. This means that cocreation is key when marketing to Millennial consumers because they expect to be involved in every part of the creation process. In return, they will essentially market the brand themselves by sharing with their friends and promoting the product on their personal pages.

⊃ **Now it's personal.** Millennials are personalizing *everything*. From their style to their technology to the way they parent, there is no singular description of this up-and-coming demographic. The key to winning with Millennials, especially new parents, is to create a brand experience that they can personalize to meet their needs. If you can also offer them a way to express their personal creativity that will help advance the brand. The combination of technology and personalization creates a way for brands to tap into two of the strongest Millennial desires and generate conversations that lead to brand loyalty.

⊃ **Of the people, by the people, for the people.** Like Honest Abe said, democracy is a philosophy that is rooted in the belief that the governing body must be of the people, by the people, and for the people. This concept has now been expanded to include the marketing industry. In 2015, brands are no longer the only stakeholders in the advertising game. Now it is the consumers who are directing the flow of conversation. Not only do they hold brands to more inclusive standards but they also expect the best service, products, and technology to be readily available to everyone at any moment.

⊃ **#Bechill.** Although Millennials did not start the casualization trend, they are certainly leaving their mark when it comes to the casualization of language. Abbreviated words, texting shorthand, and new slang have all led to shorter and more concise marketing messages. The creation of the hashtag has also led to a revolution in the organization of online digital content. Considered the new URL, hashtags are now part of every marketing strategy and are considered to be just as important as the actual company website.

⊃ **Protect self-identity.** Millennials value brands that allow them to express their own personality instead of conforming to an already defined brand stereotype. As Millennials become parents, the idea of protecting self-identity becomes even more important. Ultimately, a brand story becomes "our story" not "your story." According to the 2014 BabyCenter report, the typical Millennial mom has thirteen fewer hours to herself after having children. Brands that enable her to embrace her new motherhood while still protecting and strengthening her self-identity will see extremely positive feedback.

CHAPTER 3

Fifty Shades of Your Brand

You've heard about the concept of love, right? Love goes like this: You meet someone, you date, you have chemistry and passion that create excitement, you fall in love, you settle down, and maybe you live happily ever after. Unfortunately, when the passion wears off and things get stagnant, you oftentimes break up. Of course, the goal of any relationship is to maintain that sweet spot between passion and settling down—a balance of the excitement of passion and the stability and comfort of creating a home and a life together. This same goal holds true for the relationship between brands and consumers. As seen through the lens of New York–based BERA Brand Management, keeping the tension between dating and love is key for any brand because it allows that brand to continue to be an essential part of life that consumers *want* to interact with.

Creating Brand Passion

According to BERA, Target is one of the brands that has created a strong presence with Millennial parents, which has landed it a place on the list of most loved brands, finding and maintaining that sweet spot between dating and love. How has it landed this coveted position? By adapting to the lifestyle of Millennial parents. Despite the large-scale system hack of Target's database in 2013, YouGov Brand Index shows that satisfaction with the brand has remained consistent and relatively high, even during and after the controversial 2013 holiday season. As we know, Millennial parents are very digitally driven and are frequent online shoppers. The Cartwheel Target app features push notifications that let parents know what specials are running in the store and provides content that Millennial parents want to engage with, such as what the top mommy bloggers are putting in their carts. Target also recently attempted to gain awareness and drive Millennial sales by creating a second screen mobile site and website that let consumers purchase products shown in an episode of the TBS television show *Cougar Town*. The goal of the campaign was to show Target products in the context of an actual home and then allow viewers to purchase the products they liked instantly on the second site. This type of engagement is relatively new, and brands are still trying to figure out how to engage consumers in real time. (You'll read more about real-time content engagement in Chapter 4.)

Millennial parents in the Under Stress orbit especially respond well to product placement advertising in their favorite TV shows. For an Under Stress parent, seeing a product in a movie or TV show reassures them that the product is worth the money. Even beyond that, Under Stress Millennial parents as well as Image First parents are more likely to try a brand or product they have never used before if they see a character on TV using that same product. Similarly, parents in the Against the Grain orbit notice brand-name products featured or displayed in their favorite TV shows. Target clearly adapted to these preferences and saw extremely positive feedback as a result. Brand consulting and research organization YouGov America, which monitors daily consumer brand perceptions for more than 1,500 brands, found that Millennial parents rank Target as one of the brands they are most satisfied with compared to other retail options like T.J.Maxx, Bed Bath & Beyond, and Costco.

Brand love can come and go quickly, especially among Millennials. Ryan Barker, managing partner at BERA Brand Management shares this comment: "In the olden days, we measured brand loyalty or brand affinity with tried and true measurements like brand awareness, preference, and satisfaction. If someone had heard of your brand and had positive perceptions of it, you were on the right track to generating sales and loyalty. However, that method is missing important components that are essential to connecting with millennials—brands that are unique and meaningful."

To feed and satisfy that sweet spot of brand passion, Millennials are enthusiastic seekers of the meaningfully unique, desiring something that connects them to your brand. In order to engage young adults, the conversation must be authentic and have a genuine connection to the everyday lifestyle of a young adult. Think about it: Would you rather listen to what someone else is interested in or have a two-way conversation about something both of you can relate to?

The desire for conversational engagement has changed the way the market is creating messages designed to initiate interactions between Millennials. Barker explains that the success of a brand cannot just be defined by its financial success today. "Ninety-seven percent of brands in the U.S. that are most loved by millennials outperform the S & P 500. It's not enough to be the number one brand in your category; those measures can be misleading to marketers and give them a false sense of security based on optimism." Bud Light is a great example of a brand that is number one in its category (light beer), but the category itself has been declining over the past few years, especially among Millennials. "To be the number one guy in a sinking ship doesn't really help you," Barker comments. With Millennials, and Millennial parents in particular, the appeal of your brand has to go beyond the products you are selling and into much more emotional territory. Barker puts it in perspective by asking us to consider: "Where does your brand fall in the world of all brands in the zero sum game of mind, heart, and wallet? That is where there are invaluable learnings."

Creating passion for your brand engages Millennials in a way that allows you to achieve both short-term stickiness and long-term devotion.

Here's how to inspire brand love in eight simple steps:

1. **Cocreate products and services.** It's not just your brand anymore. It belongs to the consumers who are no longer a passive target audience but your consumer partners or "prosumers." They will determine how successful your

brand will be based on how much you involve them in the creation process.

2. **Leverage technology with brand authority.** Act to your brand's strong suits, and develop an authority in a specific space that consumers recognize and respect. Then create interactive content and technology that involve and inspire consumers.

3. **Be authentic.** Be honest and genuine because—let's be real—in the digital age, there are no secrets.

4. **Be transparent.** This goes along with authenticity. Millennials expect brands to own their flaws in addition to their successes.

5. **Be a conscious capitalist.** Although cause marketing is a big win for Millennials, it is not enough. Now Millennial brand partners expect companies to work for more than just their bottom line in every aspect of the business.

6. **Embrace brand partners.** Remember in *Finding Nemo* when Bruce the shark swore by the axiom "Fish are friends not food"? Millennials are not your meal ticket to success; they are your consumer partners in creating a shared brand experience. When you work on their terms you'll likely increase their interest in your product.

7. **Earn Millennial employee love.** Employees are your greatest stakeholders. They can either be your biggest fans or your worst enemies. Brands that embrace Millennial culture (think about Google here) will be considered a favorite and will win with the next generation. Few, if any, great brands that don't first win with Millennial employees win with Millennials consumers. So treat them well.

8. **Build energy.** What good is your brand if there is no fuel to keep it going? Building energy around your brand by producing interactive content and individualized messages keeps consumers excited and your brand top of mind.

While it would be ideal to create a campaign that touches on every one of these eight steps, the reality is that it is nearly impossible to create the perfect brand. The goal is not to accomplish each of these steps but, rather, to learn where your sweet spot is and enhance it so that it becomes the focus of your brand. The most successful brands are constantly reevaluating and reimagining what their brands look like through these lenses in order to inspire and win greater Millennial Brand Love™ and passion.

Consumers Are the Competition

One of the driving forces behind achieving brand passion is understanding your direct and indirect competitors. Watch out for the little guy—the brands you probably don't expect to take over are the ones that can potentially be your biggest threat. If consumers begin to fall out of love with your brand, there are two potential ways to deal with it: Reengage them quickly or prepare for divorce. We have seen this happen on many occasions, but one of the most notable cases of marketing divorce among Millennials is cable television. Online videos have been hugely popular with the Millennial generation and have influenced the way Millennials are watching their favorite TV shows. According to a *New York Times* survey of 4,000 online video users, 34 percent of Millennials who watch online videos watch almost no broadcast TV at all (compared to 20 percent of

Gen Xers and 10 percent of Boomers).[1] That is *one-third* of an entire demographic lost!

Convenience is a huge factor in the decision to switch from cable to online video streaming subscriptions. Millennials often think about products through the mindset of "I want what I want, when I want it, how I want it." They are also a highly on-the-go generation, even more so when they are parents, and they value brands that adapt to their busy lifestyles. Netflix, the world's leading Internet television network, took convenience to a whole new level when it was introduced in 1997, and it has since grown to serve almost 50 million subscribers internationally, gaining upward of 4 million subscribers in a single quarter.[2] Why are Millennials flocking to video streaming sites like Netflix instead of traditional cable TV? Simple—Netflix, unlike cable, is available from almost any platform where the Internet is available. Not to mention the 24/7 video streaming options, customized recommendations, affordable monthly price, and door-to-door delivery service for any physical movie rental.

> As the mother of a 2-year old, Robin doesn't have as much time to watch TV as she used to, and when she does watch it, it's on her terms. "We had cable, but I didn't have a lot of time to watch TV to make it really worth using it. When we decided that I was going to stay home from work we were looking at some bills that we could cut out and that seemed like a pretty easy one to get rid of. Now, we have Apple TV and we stream our TV through Hulu, Netflix, and Amazon. I can watch shows at my convenience—start a season of something and just watch the episodes when I want, no commercials, I can pause it. I

know you can do that with TiVo but I thought Apple TV was a cheaper alternative."

Netflix is creating brand love among Millennial parents by repositioning itself as a family entertainment brand through an exclusive deal to make recently released Disney movies available through its service starting in 2016. Netflix is also enterprising a multiyear deal with DreamWorks Animation to add more than 300 hours of programming to its service, which gives it the authority to create original content using established DreamWorks characters (think Shrek, Kung Fu Panda, and Madagascar). "Animated content reaches kids at a variety of ages, and the kids' offering is very important to us because it's a way to increase the value of our service," says Cindy Holland, vice president of original content for Netflix.[3]

This strategy aligns with the entertainment behaviors of Millennial parents. According to the 2014 BabyCenter report released by BabyCenter 21st Century Mom® Insights Series, Millennial moms are more likely than their Gen X parents to have an online video streaming subscription that they use in their homes. Additionally, only 46 percent of Millennial moms even have cable TV subscriptions, compared to 90 percent of Gen X moms.[4] Although cable television is still in high demand with the overall general public, it has teetered toward boredom and divorce within the Millennial parent demographic.

When examining competitive threats, Michael E. Porter's five forces analysis (see Figure 3–1) can be a powerful framework that goes beyond the obvious rivals to include the impact that customers, suppliers, potential entrants, and substitute products can have on a company's profitability and potential for success.

Each of these forces contributes to the competitive intensity and

FIGURE 3–1   Porter's five forces.

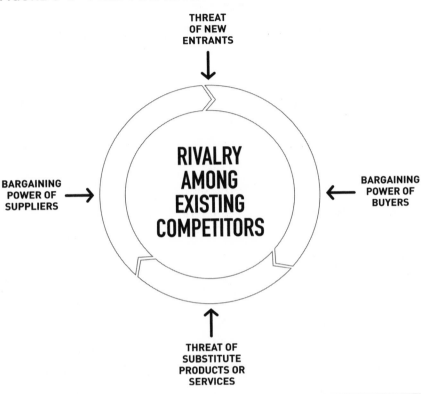

potential profitability of an industry, which ultimately reveals the attractiveness of a market. This model can be used for new organizations trying to enter a market or mature organizations wanting to better identify the competitive landscape for strategic planning.

Let's look at this model using the baby food industry as an example to better understand each of these forces:

Rivalry among existing competitors. There are several major players in the baby food industry that have been around from (what seems like) the beginning of time: Gerber, Beech-Nut, and Carnation. More recent entrants, such as Earth's Best, which has been around for twenty-five years, made a splash with a more organic, nutritious focus on baby food.

Threat of new entrants. While there are several key players in this category, as parents' needs and priorities are changing, more and more niche baby foods have hit the market, often focusing on organic, local, sustainable foods, including Plum Organics and Yummy Spoonfuls.

Bargaining power of suppliers. The suppliers of the baby food brands are the farmers and producers of the products used to make the formulas and packaged goods. There is an abundance of producers; however, the majority of the bargaining power remains with the major companies, as they have the option to source outside of the United States or leverage cheaper work from other farms. Additionally, manufacturers focused on organic baby food are up against the high (and rising) costs of organic fruits and vegetables. Suppliers for smaller and organic chains often are more involved in the process and require more attention, as the selling point of the product is highly dependent on them and the ingredients used in the baby food.

Threat of substitute products or services. There is no question that baby food is a necessity—I mean, come on, you've gotta feed babies—but parents are finding alternative methods to nourish and feed their young ones. The biggest threat from a substitute or alternate product is homemade baby food, which appeals to many Millennial parents' sense of environmentalism and desire for purer foods. One can even purchase an "as seen on TV" Baby Bullet (by the makers of the widely popular Magic Bullet), which helps parents easily make and package their own baby food.

Bargaining Power of Buyers. With pressure on the Millennial mom to be able to "do it all," some women of this generation feel obliged to make their own baby food. With that, mommy blogs, articles, and products designed to aid them in that task and help them feel like the best moms they can be put more of the bargaining power in their hands when it comes to what they will, or won't, buy. The consumer shift toward cleaner eating has, no doubt, impacted the direction of the organic and nutritious baby food movement. What will be next?

It's worth reiterating that the power of mommy blogs and the infinite access Millennial parents have to online resources have generated a drive for transparency that we have not seen in the past. Parents are now looking for products with fewer ingredients, more vitamins, and much less processing. In addition, they want to feel personally connected to their baby food brands because these brands are directly affecting the most valuable relationship for any parent. These are not new trends, but Millennial parents are creating a new culture of parenting that is founded on authenticity, transparency, and connections, which are at the core of the Millennial

Mindset. The influence and energy that Millennial parent consumers can generate for a brand, or about an industry, have impacted the way we should be looking at these forces, particularly as they relate to the relationship among the threat of new entrants, the bargaining power of buyers, and the threat of substitute products or services. This is a result of a new form of digital disintermediation. (It's too bad we don't get paid by the syllable for using words like that!) Essentially, digital disintermediation explains how the heightened use of digital and mobile technology has closed the gap between consumers and producers and reversed the flow of the conversation. Traditionally, marketers spoke to consumers. Now consumers are the ones leading the conversation and are central to how the five forces in the Porter model shape the marketing industry.

In the traditional Porter model, the rivalry among competitors was at the center of it all; keeping an eye on the competition and offering competitive services and prices was central to industry relevance. In today's competitive environment, consumers can be your biggest advocates, but they can also instigate alternate solutions. Let's go back to the baby food industry example to see this in play. Back in the day, the baby food brands dictated what was healthy for a child. Now, the DIY trend among Millennial parents, fueled by platforms like Pinterest and Instagram, is responsible for the change in the conversation model and disrupting the industry in a way that could never have happened before.

With the bargaining power of the buyer still central to these competitive forces, the threat of substitute products or services relies heavily on consumer influence. Millennials are creative and resourceful and have completely reimagined what nutrition means. Nutrition is no longer just about eating healthy. It is an entire lifestyle adjustment that starts at infancy for the children of Millennial parents. The reimagination of competition in the participation economy is a result of key Millennial trends that are completely altering the baby food industry in the same way they have influenced the marketing game.

THE REIMAGINATION

of how competition is defined in a participation economy is a result of key Millennial trends that are completely altering the baby food industry in the same way they have influenced the marketing game.

Storyliving

If there is one thing we have pushed in this book, it is that brands must stand for more than just their bottom line. What we haven't done is explain what that means. To stand for more than just your bottom line, one best-practice strategy is to act as a conscious capitalist in all facets of the business. But, more than that, you must develop not just the "what" of your business—the products you make or the services you provide—but also the "why." Why do you do what you do? Why do you believe in what you believe in? As soon as you have established your "why" you can begin sharing your story with consumers and develop a brand authority. Simon Sinek introduced his concept of developing the "why" in his TED Talk in 2009 and has since inspired thousands of leaders and hundreds of brands to reimagine their brand structure. Ultimately, successful brands embrace the idea of Storyliving™, which means that they live and breathe their story because it is a part of their core essence. What they stand for is present in the brand personality. In order to better understand Storyliving, let's take a look at one of the most successful companies that embraces its story in every interaction, message, and piece of content it creates: TOMS Shoes.

TOMS was founded in 2006 after Blake Mycoskie traveled to a small village in Argentina and found that the villagers had no shoes to protect their feet. In an effort to "create something that matters," Mycoskie started a company that gave one pair of shoes away to someone in need for every pair of shoes it sold. This trademarked one-for-one model revitalized the giving process and created a for-profit company that stands for more than its bottom line. Since then, TOMS has expanded into a multi-million-dollar company, which has provided new shoes to more than 10 million people and delivered eye care to more than 150,000 people. There are dozens of companies that support similar projects all over the world. What is it about TOMS that has made it stand out so much? Everyone who works for, purchases, or engages with TOMS lives the brand story when they purchase TOMS products.

One of the biggest draws for a Millennial to interact with a brand is whether that brand is adding value not just to the consumer's life but also to the global (or local) community. Joint research by FutureCast and Boston Consulting Group found that 56 percent of Millennial parents believe that big businesses have the financial and technological resources to help solve social problems. The brands that are doing this well have greater success with word-of-mouth marketing and experience higher rates of Millennial participation with the brand online. Overall, Millennials want to make a difference and be involved in organizations that add goodness to the world, and they are more likely to seek out and interact with the brands that are doing just that.[5]

According to the same research, 55 percent of Millennials in general have a better impression of a company that engages in programs that support causes or charities. This number increases for Millennial parents (62 percent), as they want to be good role models for their children and teach them how to give back. "It's great to see companies that give back, like TOMS. I think more highly of companies that do this than a company like McDonald's. It shows me that they care more than just about making their money or making a profit," says Millennial parent Robin. Robin is not the only Millennial parent who favors brands that sponsor philanthropic endeavors. Forty-five percent of Millennial dads and 36 percent of Millennial moms feel that they can contribute to causes or charities they care about more easily through a company's program than on their own. TOMS has cornered the market on the philanthropic for-profit business model and has completely changed the giving-back consumer culture. For Millennial parents, the option to make a purchase from a brand that supports causes like TOMS vs. a brand that does not is a no-brainer.

To perpetuate what the brand stands for, TOMS embraces customers who purchase their shoes or eyewear, including them in a special community. They are encouraged to share their photos, stories, and experiences with each other in order to raise awareness and make connections all over the world. The company also does more than just ask for monetary donations through product purchases; it invites customers into the TOMS world. TOMS has created a culture where profit and philanthropy work in a symbiotic partnership that completely aligns with everything Millennials believe in. Those who are invited into and included in this community share with their friends who are not yet involved, and almost instantly we see the reach and bandwidth of the brand expand exponentially. For example, Friends of TOMS is a nonprofit subsidiary of the for-profit company that was created in order to give customers who wanted to do more for the cause a space to do so. With the goals of mobilizing, connecting, and empowering young adults, the nonprofit enhances the TOMS brand because it provides Millennials with the opportunities to make an even greater difference in the world.

By living its story, a brand has a greater capability to develop an authoritative Brand Stand. Unlike a company's mission statement, a Brand Stand is a short, concise, pointed message that encompasses the entire brand ecosystem. A company's Brand Stand answers the question "How do I treat everything around me?" It is the foundation on which every message, piece of content, interaction, and business decision is based. For example, Chipotle's Brand Stand is "food with integrity." As we discussed in Chapter 2, Chipotle reaches Millennial consumers through shareworthy content and highly participative brand engagement strategies. However, the Brand Stand is the guacamole to the burrito, if you will; it enhances Millennial brand passion by creating a truly inviting and livable brand story. In three words, Chipotle has described its core belief and expressed to consumers everything it stands for. Best of all, there is not an "and" in the Chipotle Brand Stand, which further strengthens the very concentrated focus of the brand.

Traditionally, the Brand Stand did not hold much weight when it came to connecting with consumers. The old model was predominantly focused on the facts of the products or, rather, the function the product served in the life of the consumer. As product positioning evolved, emotion was factored into the messaging, followed by participation, and, finally, the overall brand purpose was used in the consumer message. For example, a traditional sales pitch for a vacuum was "Buy our vacuum; it will help you clean your house." Then, after marketers realized there was an emotional aspect in play, the new sales pitch became "Buy our vacuum; having a clean house will make you feel like a good parent." Later, after participation was introduced into the marketing game, the pitch became "Using feedback from young parents, we've created a new vacuum that will help you keep your home in order so you can focus on more important things." Fast-forward to 2014, when brands are developing their Brand Stands, and the message becomes "Good parents make a difference."

We can see in Figures 3–2 and 3–3 how the new Brand Stand model breaks away from focusing on the superficial benefits of a product and instead offers consumers an authentic message that gets to the core of what the company really stands for. This allows brands to establish stronger relationships and build more loyalty with their brand partners. Ultimately, brand positioning as we knew it in the past is dead and is being replaced by Brand Stands that function as unique selling propositions (USPs). However, instead of describing how the functional benefits of the product make it stand out, brands are using their Brand Stands to describe how their core values align with consumer values. In the past, a USP answered the question "What makes my product different?" However, this question does not carry much relevance—there are millions of "different" products in the market. Now the question needs to be "How does this product make the consumer feel?" or, better yet, "How does this product contribute to a stronger sense of belonging?" Think about your Brand Stand and how it answers these questions. As soon as brands are able to answer these questions, they develop brand authority that translates across all markets, as opposed to just "How is my product different from other products in my market?"

FIGURE 3–2   Brand Stand—old model.

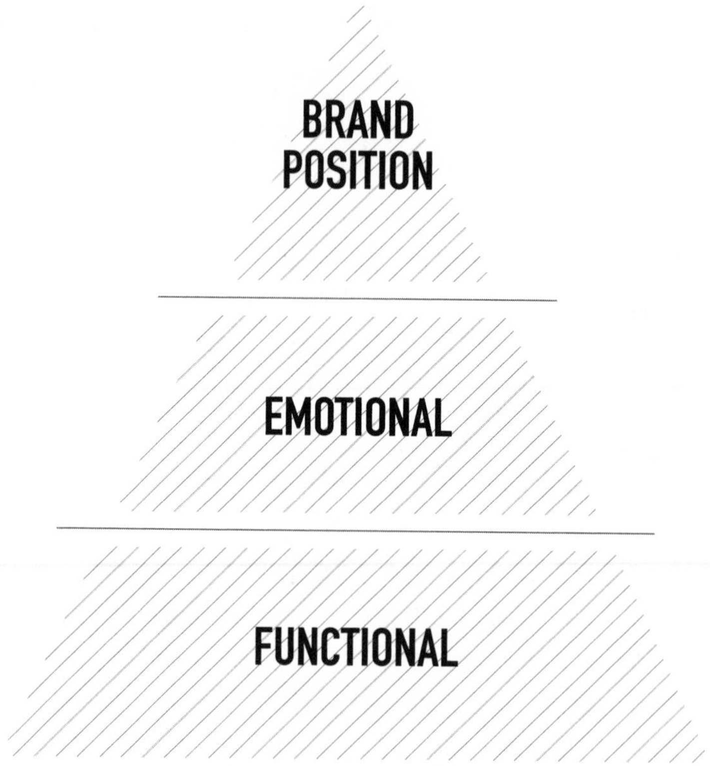

A key part of the Brand Stand is acting like a conscious capitalist. As we mentioned at the very beginning of this book (remember, way back in the Introduction?), conscious capitalism is more than just aligning your brand with a charity or participating in philanthropic events. Acting as a conscious capitalist is standing for more than just your bottom line. It is understanding how your brand, your company, your organization, your entire brand ecosystem bring value and add good to the community. Even more than that,

FIGURE 3-3 Brand Stand—new model.

it is about understanding how everything you do adds value to our world. Seem a little altruistic? Sure it is. But remember that we're dealing with Millennials here, and they are convinced they can leave this world in better condition than what they inherited. This is not an easy concept to grasp. It takes time to reimagine your brand ecosystem and make a profit while also adding "good" to the system.

Brand Stands connect with Millennials on a foundational basis

YOUR BRAND STAND SHOULD ANSWER

How does this product make the consumer feel?
How does this product contribute to a stronger sense of belonging?

because Millennials want to engage with brands that are transparent and authentic. Essentially, brands that live their Brand Stands have a greater chance of winning with Millennials. Especially as they take on parenthood, Millennials want to share their favorite brands' stories with their children, so they expect more than just traditional messaging focused on functionality and superficial benefits. Millennial parents are viewing brands through a pragmatic lens. Your Brand Stand should answer these questions: (1) How does this product make the consumer feel? and (2) How does this product contribute to a stronger sense of belonging?

Useful Is the New Cool

A funny thing happens when Millennials become parents and veer toward pragmatism: What they consider to be "cool" changes. We already know that all Millennials love convenience and have a high expectation of easy access to information. Ultimately, what is useful to Millennials actually becomes *cool*.

Useful is the new cool™.

Write that one down; it's a keeper that really captures a major Millennial consumer trend. This statement is true of all Millennials, parents or not, but Millennial parents approach technology differently than those digital natives who are not yet parents. Technology's role in the lives of Millennial parents, who often have little money and no time to spare, shifts from early adoption of the newest gadget to finding tools that simplify their lives. Their technological proclivity paired with growing pragmatism makes Millennial parents ripe for solution-oriented digital platforms that help simplify and streamline life.

A recent survey conducted by Weber Shandwick and KRC Research about Millennial moms as digital influencers found that some Millennial moms would do anything in exchange for help in managing their lives. One-quarter of moms who participated in the survey indicated that they would pay $50 per month to have someone manage their busy lives, and one in five would pay $150 per month. This price tag is twice as much as non-Millennial moms are willing to pay. For one-third, it's the sheer lack of time that is an issue; they would create time management platforms for themselves—if they had the time.[6] Elizabeth Rizzo, senior vice president for reputation research at Weber Shandwick, tells us, "We think there are two possible reasons that Millennial moms' interest in paying for 'life management outsourcing' is higher than that of moms overall . . . either Millennial moms lead more harried lives, or perhaps, they are just more willing to spend on assistance than generations before them."

So if they are willing to pay that much, what about a free app that simplifies the food buying process? Coupons.com, which controls 90 percent of the digital coupon market,[7] released the Grocery iQ app designed to simplify grocery shopping. This popular app allows the user to build grocery lists from a database of millions of items by typing, voice searching, or scanning bar codes. From there, users can organize their lists by aisle as well as track the history of their lists. Users can easily search for coupons and nearby stores from the app.

For busy parents, this creates solutions that go well beyond solving the problem of how to spend time in the grocery store more efficiently. Parents can easily keep track of household staples and identify their own purchasing habits that are not cost efficient. Most important, this app helps parents plan their meals so they do not have to reinvent the wheel (of meal planning) every week. There's an added benefit for parents like Emily who share the grocery shopping responsibilities with their spouse: "I find Grocery IQ incredibly useful. We are both logged on and can enter items we need to get as we run out, so whoever goes has the whole list."

Another sharing app that enables families to work together to monitor household spending is Mint. Mint streamlines household budgeting and financial management by pulling all financial information and accounts into one place, using one password to provide a holistic view of the family's financial situation. Purchased by Intuit in 2009, Mint has grown to encompass more than 10 million users. Mint faced several challenges to growth when it was initially developed, the first being that finances are not necessarily "sexy." Many Millennials see saving and budgeting as a chore—something they have to do, not something they want to do. Furthermore, the site asks users to make all of their financial information available to a young company—something Millennials are not so keen on doing.

The founder of Mint, Aaron Patzer, had a plan to target, engage, and ultimately create trust among consumers, many of them Millennials. For Mint, the combination of doing market research, creating a superior product, and generating buzz through content marketing was the recipe for success.

Market research comes in many shapes, sizes, and budgets. It can be as formal as conducting focus groups or web surveys or as informal as crowdsourcing an idea and getting feedback from anyone and everyone. Guess which one Patzer did? When he initially asked people how they would feel about an online budgeting site, only 1 out of almost 100 people showed interest in using a financial website like this. After refining the concept and writing several alternate messages, including "Mint is your Money Ninja" and "Mint is your Money Champion," he took it to the train station to find the best messaging. This type of crowdsourcing method is extremely well aligned with the Millennial Mindset. Millennials themselves often use crowdsourcing as a method of gaining brand information, so brands that partake in the same activity rank higher among Millennials and Millennial parents. Knowing that security was going to be a primary barrier to usage, he also tested messaging around security. The term "bank-level security" resonated so strongly that, to this day, it is highlighted on Mint's website.

Patzer believes that, when creating a business such as this, you should validate your idea early and thoroughly. In an interview with Princeton Academics, Patzer explained that he did not initially write any code for the Mint program. Instead, he spent a significant amount of time fully baking the idea before jumping into the coding process. While some professionals argue the best method is to begin with coding in order to establish a prototype, Patzer disagrees: "[Rapid prototyping] works for certain types of things; I think anything that is social . . . that works. But for finance I wanted to be a little more rigorous and there were a lot of technical problems, connectivity to all of the banks, and the business model."[8]

Another challenge was the competitive landscape. Other financial management software was available, and those companies had much deeper pockets than Mint. Product differentiation was key to competing in this market. Patzer approached this issue by leveraging the weaknesses of the competition to create a superior product. With a much quicker setup time, a stronger algorithm to minimize the number of uncategorized expenses, and financial planning tools that provide simple answers to questions such as how much money to save for retirement, children's college, or big-ticket items, Mint was born.

It was time to push out the marketing strategy. The early marketing strategy had a simple, if not challenging, goal: Do as much as possible to create interest, buzz, and trust for as little money as possible. Almost a full year before the product was launched, Mint focused on content marketing, using clever topics such as "Train Wreck Tuesdays," where blog contributors warned about the dangers of personal finance, and inviting high-level professionals to share what's in their wallet. By offering users who shared the "I want Mint" badge on their Facebook page VIP status when the product launched, Mint received free advertising on 600 different blogs and a search engine optimization (SEO) boost due to the links directing viewers to Mint.com. These efforts, combined with easy-to-read infographics and blog contributions by noteworthy financial bloggers, all led up to a successful launch.

In the interview, Patzer explained that the overall goal was to create a finance blog that was both personal and provided useful content for users. The primary target for Mint.com was young professionals who were not familiar with budgeting and managing household and personal finances—an audience that Patzer felt was being neglected before the site launched. Eventually the blog and app became a number one resource regarding personal finance for Millennials. The infographics and articles drove regular traffic to both the site and the app and were often featured on platforms like Digg and Reddit. By the time the site was live, Mint had more traffic than all other personal finance sites combined.[9]

Content includes advice from industry professionals about how to manage home and personal finances in addition to providing saving tips for young parents living on a budget. The Mint community also features support from the Mint staff and extremely helpful short videos that are both interactive and informative when it comes to financial education. Same of the latest articles posted to the Mint blog include "4 Survival Tips for the Working Parent," "American Family Budget: One Year Later," and "5 Money Lessons to Teach Our Daughter." All of the articles on the blog are written for and directed toward Millennials and Millennial parents (using very Millennial-centric language). The secret to Mint's success is not just the fact that it created an excellent content marketing plan, but that it created a tool that is useful for Millennial parent consumers.

Let's look at one more example in which a company has taken the concept "Useful is the new cool" to heart.

Michael's daughter, Megan, woke up at 7 a.m. complaining that her throat felt "icky" and her tummy was sore. A little milk and breakfast usually makes her feel better, so they headed to the kitchen for a bite. It wasn't long before it was clear that Megan really was sick this time and needed to get to a doctor that day. Like a good dad, Michael tucked his daughter back into bed so he could make a doctor's appointment. After calling Megan's regular pediatrician and learning that he was out of town for the next week, Michael logged in to ZocDoc.com. He had used the service a few months back, after seeing an advertisement for the page on his favorite blog, 8 Bit Dad, when he needed to go to the doctor for a similar bug. He had been extremely happy with the results of the site and hoped for the same outcome this time around with his daughter.

At ZocDoc.com, Michael typed in his insurance provider and was given a list of recommended pediatricians in his area that accepted his insurance. Better yet, he could see available appointment times as early as that afternoon as well as read reviews written by other parents. Later that afternoon, Michael took his daughter to the doctor, got some antibiotics for her and lollipops for both of them, and experienced a huge feeling of relief. Michael posted his story to Facebook so if his friends found themselves in a similar position they could benefit from his experience.

Michael is not the only happy customer of ZocDoc, a free service that allows patients to find doctors in their area that accept their insurance, book appointments, and fill out paperwork online. The company was created in 2007 after founder Cyrus Massoumi suffered from a painful ear infection and was not able to see a doctor for three weeks. Upset with the time it took to get an appointment and the service he received when he finally got in to see a doctor, Cyrus decided it was time to create a better system for people needing such medical attention. ZocDoc provides real-time schedule updates for doctors using the site—that means that when people cancel their appointments or don't show up, that availability is instantly posted to the doctor's profile page. Most people who book with ZocDoc see a doctor within twenty-four hours. Imagine how life-changing this is for a first-time parent. Have you ever had to deal with a two-year-old who had an infection? Waiting to see a doctor is that last thing you want to do.

Today, ZocDoc covers 1,600 cities (40 percent of the United States) and is growing rapidly. The majority of appointments booked are made by people between the ages of 18 and 34—our beloved Millennials. What is it about ZocDoc that makes it so appealing to Millennials, especially Millennial parents? It aligns with almost every value we've outlined for them. New parents have a busy lifestyle and are balancing the demands of family, work, and a home. Sounds pretty crazy. Anything that can help them organize their lives is a win. The ease of using ZocDoc has essentially revolutionized the way parents manage healthcare for their families.

Think about what you do when you want to book a family vacation. You jump onto Orbitz or Kayak and book your flight, hotel, and rental car all from one site. Easy. Just as these sites have reinvented the way we plan vacations, ZocDoc is rethinking the way we plan doctor's visits by making everything available on one site. It's a simple idea with a big punch, providing a unique value proposition that no other company has to offer. This site has grown in a matter of a few years because of its disruptive nature, and it has huge shareworthy potential because, frankly, it works.

Yeah, yeah, yeah, technology is great, you get it. Using technology to help Mom manage the groceries or make a doctor's appointment with an app is a great life management solution, but can it be taken too far? Integrating technology into children's products can backfire quickly when applied and marketed poorly. The controversy that erupted over Fisher-Price's Newborn-to-Toddler

Apptivity™ Seat suggests that, indeed, it can. The product itself is a reclining seat with an iPad holder positioned right over the baby's head so he or she can easily view the screen without Mom or Dad having to hold it in place. Additionally, it comes with free downloadable apps that offer soothing or educational content, based on the age of the child. Millennials love technology and kids love iPads, so it's gotta be great, right?

Not so much. Many parents were disgusted by this product and were not afraid to share that sentiment. This is an example of high participation and high shareworthiness that quickly went awry. The primary complaint is that it's just not good for children, often citing that the American Academy of Pediatrics recommends no screen time before children are at least 2 years old.[10] Of course, none cited the study of more than 1,000 parents with children between the ages of 2 months and 24 months, which found that 90 percent of parents let their children regularly watch television, DVDs, or videos.[11] I guess their children are all watching educational entertainment like StoryBots. But we digress.

The other main complaint is that it encourages lazy parenting. The Q&A section on Amazon for this product, which features consumer questions answered by consumers, reveals the concern in a humorous way:

Q: Will this toy replace parenting my two month old? His constant clamoring for attention cuts into my "me time," and I want a mini-TV for him to stare at.

A: No, you will still have to occasionally feed him and change his diaper once in a while. But I'm pretty sure Fisher-Price is working on a product to automate those chores too.

Q: I want to enhance the experience for my child, are "apptivity toothpicks" available to prop their eyes open?

A: Toothpicks are so old school. A mild electric shock is administered when child looks away.

Q: What is the weight limit?

A: About 100 lbs. This is to ensure your child can gain an excess amount of weight at a very young age, thus ensuring he/she will never need to walk.

Q: Will my child go to Harvard if I buy this product?

A: No, they'll be stuck going to Yale.[12]

All joking aside, the reviews on Amazon are telling, with a whopping 71 percent giving only one out of five stars. Based on the content of these reviews, it doesn't look like many (or any) of the reviewers actually bought the product in question. Ouch.

Some are taking a more proactive approach. The Campaign for a Commercial-Free Childhood (CCFC) petitioned to get the Apptivity Seat recalled, claiming more than 12,000 signatures from parents, grandparents, educators, and health professionals.[13] The CCFC's director, Dr. Susan Linn, is concerned with the product itself, as well as Fisher-Price's credibility. Dr. Linn explained that the Apptivity Seat discourages social interactions that are critical for the learning and health development of young infants. In an interview, Dr. Linn said, "Fisher-Price is damaging its reputation as a brand parents can trust. They should pull the plug on the Apptivity Seat and go back to the drawing board."

In response to all of the controversy, Fisher-Price posted a note on its site to address the previous concerns. The note assured customers that the company appreciates and values feedback from consumers. The note recommended that parents using the Apptivity Seat do so with limitations regarding viewing time and appropriate content. The note closed reminding customers that the Apptivity Seat is only one of the many baby seats that the company produces.

What about the old adage that all publicity is good publicity? In this day and age, when information can be spread quickly and in large volume to live forever on the Internet, perhaps not.

When it comes to utility, the goal is to answer the question "Can I live without this?" If the answer is yes, then you are not addressing the key issue. Parents who want to use technology to help them better raise their children want a product that is safe and reliable and that makes them feel like good parents. Where ZocDoc succeeded was in tapping into one of the most stressful aspects of being a new parent: child medical care. No family can live without it. In contrast, Fisher-Price failed because not only did it create a product that was not imperative for a child's upbringing, but it did so in an arguably harmful way. Brands must remember that, although useful is the new cool, products must address the right questions in order to create a product that is truly useful.

CHAPTER 3: KEY TAKEAWAYS

- ⟳ **Keep the balance between comfort and passion.** The relationship between a brand and a consumer, just like relationships between people, takes a lot of work. Knowing where the sweet spot is and creating a healthy balance between comfort and passion is key. Open lines of communication and new interactive campaigns will keep things fresh and innovative while continuing to strengthen the relationship.

- ⟳ **Brains over brawn.** New companies can pack quite the punch and oftentimes have little equity in old schemas. Brands that are disruptive and offer customers a new experience have the potential to take out even the most well-known and successful brands (keep in my mind how Dollar Shave Club forced Gillette to rethink its entire business model). If you are a mature brand, consider acting like a disruptor brand by leaving room in your budget to take risks.

- ⟳ **Storyliving leads to authority.** Brands that have a strong "why" and create a product that people can believe in will win with Millennials. Now, more than ever, consumers do not want to be told about a brand. They want to live it. They want to experience it. Brands that are able to live their story and bring active consumer partners into the process will develop a strong brand personality that will establish an authority and point of view that can be shared beyond just their industry category. Your most loyal customers will believe in what you do, not just what you sell.

- ⟳ **How can you help me make my life better, faster, simpler, _____?** *(Fill in the blank.)* Technology is expected, but utility is rewarded. Millennials grew up with parents who controlled every aspect of their lives. While Millennial parents are significantly less controlling than their own parents were, they are still looking for brands that bring them that same organizational structure. Brands that leverage technology to make life easier will win in a Millennial-driven economy. American pragmatism as we now know it focuses on how brands can utilize technology to solve problems and help manage families. Millennial parents are the do-it-all generation. They have a job, they have a social life, and, on top of all of that, they have a family. Useful is the new cool when defining products and services offered to Millennials.

CHAPTER 4

The Power of Energy

You are more than halfway through this book, so you know by now that some of the traditional business models that you learned in school or in your years in the industry have to be altered or revamped to apply to the Millennial market (such as Porter's five forces, discussed in Chapter 3). The habits, preferences, and behaviors of Millennials are changing the market, so it's time to forget about it—unlearn what you know and embrace a new framework to engage Millennial parents.

The Path to Purchase

Let's look at another model. This time, we are going to break down the AIDA model. You know this one—AIDA describes the series

FIGURE 4–1 AIDA—old model.

ACTION

DESIRE

INTEREST

AWARENESS

of events a consumer goes through when exposed to advertising and marketing. (See Figure 4–1.)

As an example, let's say you run a local children's consignment clothing store. Your marketing strategy is to make consumers aware of the clothing you sell, make them want it, and then get them to come to your store and buy it. It's simple enough—a linear process of consumer engagement. Let's go back in time (pre-Millennial and pre-Internet) to see how the AIDA model used to work:

Barbara has been frustrated by how quickly her children outgrow their clothing—it costs an arm and a leg to keep those kids dressed! While sorting through the mail, she comes across a flyer for your store, a children's consignment clothing store. Funny, she was just thinking there had to be a better option than constantly buying new clothes and donating them to Goodwill.—you have her *awareness*. The flyer depicts an image of happy kids showing off their new outfits and a very happy mom holding fistfuls of cash. Barbara wants to be that mom—you have her *interest*. It's not quite clear from the flyer how the consignment and store credits work, so she gives the store a call. On her landline. (Remember, we've gone back in time a bit.) She asks a few questions, and the friendly and knowledgeable sales associate piques her *desire*. She gets the kids dressed in their too-small clothes, grabs the most recent load of unfolded clean laundry, and heads out to the store to start consigning. There's your *action*.

If you can get past the landline portion of this example, you can see how this linear model made perfect sense back in the day. But now let's look at the same example using a Millennial mom:

Jessica has been frustrated by how quickly her children grow out of their clothing—it costs an arm and a leg to keep those kids dressed! (Sound familiar?) She goes to Facebook to reach out to her mom friends to find out if it is just her, or if other moms are having the same problem. She gets comments from almost forty other moms who live in her area. With her entrepreneurial spirit, Jessica sees an opportunity. She goes to Google and searches

"What does it take to start a consignment shop from my home?" She finds "consignment shops near me" on her smartphone and calls a few to learn more about the process of consignment. She then watches a YouTube series about how to be more entrepreneurial and how to start your own business. The series has more than 5,000 views, so she decides it is legitimate and begins taking the steps to create her own business. Within a month, "Jess's Baby Closet" has a Facebook page and her first event has more than 100 RSVPs (thanks to her friends rallying to the cause). All the while, the flyer for your children's consignment shop has gone straight from Jessica's mailbox to her recycle bin.

Not only did your store not even catch Jessica's attention, but she found your store on her own and used the information about your store in a way you hadn't imagined. It's important to remember that Millennial moms are incredibly entrepreneurial—we like to call them "mompreneurs." According to the BabyCenter report, more than half of all 1,353 Millennial moms surveyed want to start their own business. This report also found that Millennial moms are 17 percent more likely to freelance and that 39 percent have used social media to sell items they personally have made.[1] This means that just capturing their attention with a good idea is not enough. Without gaining her awareness in a way that fits her lifestyle, your store didn't even get the chance to be considered.

Although not spelled out in the AIDA model, it's safe to assume that the outcome of applying this model, after the consumer takes action (or purchases something), is that the consumer feels fulfillment or excitement about the purchase and, ideally, shares that joy with others, spreading the word. In Barbara's example, maybe she felt a sense of relief at having found the store and left it feeling like a smart shopper and a good mom. With Jessica, however, the excitement and idea sharing happened throughout the entire process. She was not excited about a purchase, or even about your specific store, but she engaged her peer group early and often, and created buzz before there was anything to buzz about.

The AIDA model focuses on what your company or brand needs to do to gain consumer engagement, but this does not reflect the market anymore. Now consumers don't have to wait to be informed; they can inform themselves. In fact, the path to purchase, or steps that a shopper takes when planning and buying a product, has changed drastically over time. Back when there were only three types of toothpaste to choose from and one type of store to buy them at (we're going way back here), the path to purchase was relatively simple: Go to store; pick one of three products; game over. That may be oversimplifying it a bit, but you get the gist.

Today's path to purchase model is far more comprehensive, taking the holistic shopping experience into account. We can imagine this new model as a pinball machine. The pinball method emphasizes how each piece is disconnected but still dependent on the others. According to Joe Cox, director of social media at Barkley US, "This model allows consumers to bounce from one touch point to another—not at all going in any order. In this way, it's more of a strategy about being in the right place at the right time." If we consider the Millennial consumer to be the ball, every other piece of the game becomes a touch point for the consumer. In the game, the more places the ball touches, the more points the player scores. This is similar to the situation of consumers—the more places the brand message can touch consumers (whether it's the trigger, research, channel selection, product selection, brand selection, or in-store path), the more likely they are to take action. The idea is have the ball (the consumer) in constant play so there is constant engagement. In order to better understand how this method works, let's take a look at the path to purchase today for a tube of toothpaste.

Trigger: How does she determine it's time to buy toothpaste?
- Does she need more toothpaste?
- Do her kids not like the taste of the last toothpaste she bought?
- Are her teeth sensitive to her current toothpaste?

Research: What kinds of research, if any, does she do?
- Does she ask her dentist for a recommendation of a toothpaste brand that is good for sensitive teeth?
- Does she post a question on Facebook asking other moms what type of toothpaste their kids like?
- Does she do no research?

Channel selection: How does she decide which store to go to for toothpaste?
- Is she making a trip just for toothpaste or is it part of a larger shopping trip?
- Does she choose the store based on best price? Product mix? Loyalty program?
- What is the proximity of the store to her home?

Product selection: What factors influence which product she selects?
- How does she choose between gel and paste, sensitive teeth and regular?

- What influences her choice?
- At what point in the process does she make the product decision, and how does that impact other steps?

Brand selection: How does she pick the brand?
- Does she buy the same brand she always does? Out of loyalty or fear of the unknown?
- If she tries a new brand, where does she hear about it? Does advertising or personal recommendation influence her?

In-store path: Where does she go in the store?
- Where does she physically go in the store to select her toothpaste? What does she pass along the way that impacts her decision?
- Who does she shop with, and what influence do they have?
- What information does she look for on the product packaging or at the shelf that helps her make a decision?

That (rather exhausting) example about toothpaste illustrates the complexity and intricacies of the shopper's path to purchase. The amount of selection that we have as shoppers and the easy access to information through technology have largely influenced changes to the path to purchase over the years. With Millennial moms, the integration and use of technology in this process are at an even greater level. Especially when it comes to recommendations and idea sharing, Millennial moms are more likely than other, non-Millennial moms to reach out to their networks via social media to share opinions and read what peers have to say. According to the BabyCenter report, one in five Millennial moms made a purchase because she saw someone else in her network following that brand.[2] As we look at more complicated products and bigger-ticket items—such as electronics or kids' toys, which may include an added layer of safety and/or educational value concerns—the path to purchase becomes even more convoluted and complicated. According to a survey conducted by the Intelligence Group, nearly three-fourths of Millennials do online research before shopping.[3] This means that the path to purchase is no longer linear. Millennials are taking turns left and right when it comes to finding the products they are looking for.

Center Your Energy

With this understanding of how people, particularly Millennial moms, shop, we have developed a new model—the Brand Atom model—which takes into account the fact that the consumer is proactive not only in the purchasing process but also in generating the energy surrounding your brand. (See Figure 4–2.)

The traditional AIDA model resembled Abraham Maslow's hierarchy of needs. It was necessary to fill each section of the pyramid before moving on to the one above. This way of thinking forced brands to spend thousands of dollars just building awareness of a product, as it was the foundation of the pyramid. Now, however, each component is independent and can be manipulated in conjunction with or apart from any other component. To better understand how this model works, let's break down each of the components.

Partnership

The partnership is the piece that holds the entire model together. Let's call this the gravity. Millennial parents do not want to be your

---

FIGURE 4–2   Brand Atom model.

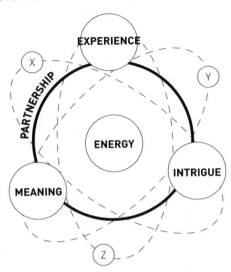

---

customers; they want to be your consumer partners. They want to interact, ask questions, offer suggestions, and cocreate the product or service, cocreate the customer journey, and cocreate the marketing. This allows them to take ownership of your product, company, and/or brand and turns them into brand ambassadors, not just consumers.

Intrigue

Intrigue is a combination of interest and desire, but it goes beyond creating curiosity by describing benefits. Rather, intrigue is more mysterious and harder to achieve. (Kind of like love, right?) This is about captivating consumers by offering something new, different, exciting, or compelling. Creating intrigue is not just about answering the question "How is your brand different from any other brand?" but answering "How can I use the brand to make my life easier, better, and more fulfilling?"

Meaning

What is one of the best ways to engage Millennials and earn their brand passion? By making a genuine difference. Brands that align with a charity, foundation, or other philanthropic organization typically have a stronger presence within the Millennial demographic. However, it must go deeper than that. Brands are expected to have these types of partnerships. Now they must act as conscious capitalists in every aspect of the business model. Millennial parents especially are more likely to interact with brands that stand for more than just their bottom lines. Brands that have a purpose and are acting based on the "why" of the company as opposed to the "how" or "what" will win with Millennials.

Experience

If we consider the "meaning" component of this model to be the consumer's perceptions and the "intrigue" to be the consumer's motivation, then the "experience" component would be the consumer's actions. The brand experience includes the interactions, conversations, and engagement between a consumer and a brand. These experiences can happen in a variety of environments and are typically fueled by content. These experiences are key because they make the brand, product, or company more memorable and, ultimately, more loved by Millennial consumers.

Energy

As you can see in the Brand Atom model (Figure 4–2), all components revolve around the energy nucleus. Unlike the AIDA model, which ends in action (purchase), the Brand Atom model doesn't focus on the moment the consumer gives you money for your product. Sure, that's still an important component of the endgame—you want people to buy your stuff—but that is not the last step or outcome by any means. Creating energy for your brand is about creating buzz—getting people talking about it, sharing content (more on Content Excellence later), and spreading their joy. Brands are no longer isolated iconic forces that "communicate" an image; they now are essentially owned by the people who use them.

This model is extremely agile and can be manipulated depending on real-time consumer feedback. Remember Jessica and her consignment shop at the beginning of this chapter? Let's take a step back and imagine what the original store (let's call it Corner Consignment) could do differently based on the Brand Atom model in order to get Jessica into the store instead of starting her own business.

> Jessica has been frustrated by how quickly her children grow out of their clothing—it costs an arm and a leg to keep those kids dressed! (Sound familiar?) She goes to Facebook to reach out to her mom friends to find out if anyone else is in a similar situation. After she posts her question, one of her mom friends, Annie, comments with a link to the Corner Consignment Facebook page explaining that she always finds great brand-name clothes at the store for half of what it would normally cost. That much of a discount? Jessica is *intrigued*. She visits the

Facebook page and sees that tons of her other mom friends also like the page and regularly post about the clothing they're selling at the store. Jessica could see there is a lot of *buzz* and good *energy* circulating about Corner Consignment and decides to check it out.

When Jessica walks into the store, she is amazed at how many options there are for children's clothing and accessories. She is also impressed by the quality of the gently worn products. (She has always been a little wary of thrift store shopping.) Walking around the store, Jessica notices there are "kids' stations" throughout the aisles. Each station has a few games, some coloring books, and other activities to help keep her rambunctious boys occupied while she shops. She asks a few of the women in the store what they think about Corner Consignment, and they all agree it is one of the better shopping *experiences* they have had with their children in tow.

Nearly convinced, Jessica asks the woman at the cash register how the consignment process works. She explains that the clothing in the store is still owned by the person selling the products, but, for each product it sells, the store takes a small percentage and the rest of the revenue goes to the owner of the clothing, ultimately supporting local moms. The woman tells her that Corner Consignment is not just a place to buy clothing; it is a place of commerce and empowerment for mothers and families in the community. Jessica appreciates the deeper *meaning* of the store, and, after learning more about the selling and buying process, her entrepreneurial spirit takes hold. As soon as she gets home, she bundles her boys, the boxes of clothes that no longer fit them, and their old stroller into the car and heads back to Corner Consignment. Jessica is convinced this will be the start of a great *partnership*.

Although this is a hypothetical example, it is clear that the Brand Atom model allows brands to think in a more engaging and agile way when it comes to interacting with Millennial consumers. In this example, Corner Consignment is able to utilize the social environments Jessica is a part of in order to gain her loyalty as a customer and consumer partner. The focus on engaging with Jessica and creating face-to-face interactions rather than just driving a purchase makes her feel she is important and worth more than just a dollar sign. This relies heavily on a brand's ability to be agile and adapt to constantly changing consumer preferences and trends.

Brand agility is a key piece in any successful marketing campaign. As technology and product innovations move our lives at a faster rate, brands must keep up with the motion and are expected to progress alongside trends, not behind them. Therefore, imagine this Brand Atom model in constant perpetual motion, meaning that the three primary orbits do not have to be equidistant from the "energy" nucleus or equal in size. It is very possible that some brands have stronger "meaning" and weaker "intrigue" components. In this instance, the "intrigue" orbit would be farther from the center. It is also important to note that this model includes smaller orbits (X, Y, Z). These orbits are completely dependent on the specific brand. For example, personalization is a very strong point of differentiation for Millennial moms. Continuing with our hypothetical example of Corner Consignment, say that the store offers personalized stations for each seller. Moms who work with Corner Consignment have the ability to design their stations any way they choose, creating a personalized retail space as a part of the overall Corner Consignment store. Therefore, the Brand Atom for Corner Consignment would also include a smaller "personalization" orbit that would stand in place of one of the X, Y, or Z orbits. When applied correctly, the Brand Atom becomes a map for companies to use to evaluate and monitor their brand in real time based on the strengths and weaknesses of a specific organization.

Not only has the path to purchase model itself changed, but also the rate at which customers go through this purchase model has drastically increased over the past decade. As technology has made information readily available, a Millennial could potentially go through this model and make multiple purchases from multiple brands within an hour. To better understand this concept, think about buying a new car. In the traditional model, one fueled by the Baby Boomer generation, customers would go to the dealership, look at different cars, test-drive a few, go to a different dealership, and do the same thing before a purchase was made. This process often took months to complete (ah, the patient Boomers). Millennials, however, are visiting fewer dealerships than ever before because information about the cars they are interested in is instantly available. Millennials may begin their search for a new car with one manufacturer in mind and, after finding new information online, completely rebuild the optimal car in their mind. And that's all before they start shopping around for the best deal!

This model also leads to a high rate of sharing. Everything that Millennial Mindset consumers do leads them to share product or brand information with their peers. According to research conducted at Oxford University Research, people don't just share facts—they share emotion. This means that your brand must be shareworthy on more than just a superficial level. This adds to the energy surrounding your brand, the intrigue drawing customers into your brand, the way people find out about the meaning of your brand, and, without question, the way Millennial customers partner with your brand. As a part of the participation economy, Millennials share essentially everything they have, know, and believe in with their networks—do not think that your brand will not be shared by a Millennial. The key is that they will share something that is good *or* bad. Millennials will post negative product reviews to their Facebook pages just as quickly as they would post positive reviews—sometimes they may post negative responses even more quickly. This means that brands must not only embrace the sharing trends that have taken over the marketing industry, but also be able to redirect those negative feelings toward something more positive. How do brands do this successfully? We're glad you asked . . .

Let's explore this new model through the ALS Ice Bucket Challenge that took over Facebook, Instagram, and Twitter newsfeeds for what seems like an inordinate amount of time for a grassroots campaign. Unless you lived under a rock for the better part of the summer of 2014, you saw the thousands of videos of people dumping ice water over their heads in an effort to raise awareness about amyotrophic lateral sclerosis (ALS), the fatal illness also known as Lou Gehrig's disease. As of August 2014, $88.5 million was raised for the ALS Association. What was it about the ALS Ice Bucket campaign that made it so successful? First of all, it wasn't a "campaign."

The Ice Bucket Challenge was originally a spinoff of the popular polar plunges, where people who were challenged either had to jump into a body of freezing-cold water or donate $100 to the charity of their choice. The exact origin of the ALS Ice Bucket Challenge has been debated, but many claim that former Boston College baseball player Pete Francis was the first to make this form of ALS donation mainstream. After being challenged himself, he nominated his pals Tom Brady and Matt Ryan to take the challenge to help #strikeoutALS. What happened next will be cited as a case study in marketing textbooks for the next decade. The entire movement went viral and did so with very little effort from the ALS Association itself. Why?

1. Think about the *partnership* aspect of the model. The Ice Bucket Challenge allows participants to partner with the organization in a way that is more engaging than writing a check. Participants who film themselves throwing ice-cold water on themselves and post the video to their Facebook page genuinely feel like they are contributing to a great cause. Especially when it comes to Millennial parents on a budget, who may not have the means to make a considerable donation, the chance to participate in raising awareness for a good cause is reason enough to get involved. Additionally, as we know, Millennials are digital natives and highly responsive to peer affirmation. The Ice Bucket Challenge is a way they can let their friends know they support the cause and ultimately receive reinforcement in the form of likes and shares.

2. Before the ALS Ice Bucket Challenge, donations came from a very close-knit group of donors who generally had a personal connection to the disease. After the challenge began, the ALS Association received donations from 145,918 new donors within a two-week period. This is

due in large part to the *intrigue* generated by the challenge itself. ALS is not a common disease and affects only 20,000 to 30,000 people in the United States. As soon as the videos started going viral and celebrities began posting their own Ice Bucket Challenge videos, people started to research ALS and jump on the Ice Bucket Challenge bandwagon in order to be a part of the drive to raise awareness and donations.

3. For nonprofit organizations, the *meaningful* component of the Brand Atom is easy to pinpoint. However, that does not mean that they are off the hook when it comes to making sure people know what the mission of the organization is. As soon as the Ice Bucket Challenge went viral, the ALS Association began creating more educational material and latched on to the awareness that was being generated by the challenge. Now nearly double the number of people compared to this same time last year know about ALS. As the Millennial generation forces brands to stand for more than their bottom line, nonprofits are not exempt from this and must stay true to their word about what they promise funds will be allocated to.

4. There is no question as to whether or not the Ice Bucket Challenge created an *experience* for participants. The key here is that is that this was not just an experience for each individual participant; it was community experience that each person who posted a video was a part of. Even those who did not make a video still shared in the experience by watching their friends, family, peers, celebrities, and even random strangers throw water on their heads.

5. Since the Ice Bucket Challenge went viral, the *energy* around the culture of giving has completely changed. The ALS Association and additional ALS funding sites have seen a tremendous increase in the awareness of what ALS is and the effects it has on the nervous system. However, people are now using the buzz around the ALS Ice Bucket Challenge to begin spreading the word about other organizations they care about. Now when people accept the challenge they are speaking not only about ALS but about other diseases and charities that mean something to them personally. In other words, the Ice Bucket Challenge is reverting to the original purpose of the polar plunge. However, it's doing so in an entirely different way than what was originally intended. Now the energy surrounding charity is stronger and has greater potential to reach a new, digitally driven Millennial audience.

This new model is a much broader approach to the consumer purchase model. It focuses more on the consumer engagement and life of the brand in general. This way of thinking puts everything Millennials value into a system that generates energy instead of an action. Although the ALS Ice Bucket Challenge was not directed toward Millennials specifically, it was very much inspired by the Millennial Mindset. The Millennial generation has orchestrated the integration of technology into the consumer and market economy, without which the ALS Challenge could never have been a success. For Millennial parents, this campaign created not only an opportunity to teach their children about giving back but also a family experience that they were encouraged to share on all social networks.

This aligns with the majority of the social behaviors of all parent orbits. Family First parents appreciate the family experience component and the ability to share that with other family and friends who could not take part, Image First parents want to share what they are doing on their networks and be part of the "in" crowd, Against the Grain and Under Stress parents appreciate the opportunity to make a difference without having to pull out their wallets, and Style and Substance parents used the challenge as a way to connect their networks and teach their children a valuable lesson.

The energy for the challenge was created organically, and the ALS foundation was able to benefit from an entirely consumer-fueled and -generated campaign. True, it was not driven by the brand itself, but this is an incredible example of the potential that lies within the Brand Atom and how brands can utilize this model to create, inspire, and engage Millennials and harness the Millennial Mindset. Comparing our hypothetical consignment store example and the ALS Ice Bucket Challenge, it is apparent that the methodology behind consumer engagement is changing in a way that is more Millennial driven and dependent on a nonlinear, more engagement-focused path to purchase. This model is about more than just getting a customer into the store; it's about creating energy surrounding a product or brand that fuels conversations, relationships, and, ultimately, an action.

If You Build the Content, They Will Come

What if we told you that social media marketing was dead? Okay, now pick your jaw up off the floor and let us explain. We are not saying social media itself is dead. It is still one of the most successful vehicles used to get a message out into the world; however, it is no longer the catalyst for action. In the participation economy, it is the content that drives action. Now, having Facebook is not enough when there is no content to be shared. Twitter means nothing unless your tweets speak to individuals. Everything that is distributed on social media must have purpose and be content driven. It is important to note that when we say "purpose" we do not mean simply the mission of "selling more products" or "making more revenue." Instead, we mean having a purpose to each specific consumer. (Hint: Think back to the Brand Stand we discussed in Chapter 3.)

The old creative excellence framework was focused on creating the perfect message and shotgunning that message out through a variety of different channels in order to reach consumers. The goal was to tell consumers about the product and inspire them to take action. But, really, when was the last time any consumer did what he or she was told, especially a Millennial consumer? The new model of Content Excellence, as we can see in Figure 4–3, is built around the idea that the traditional concept of creative excellence is only a piece of the greater Content Excellence strategy that brands should utilize today to engage Millennials and Millennial parents. While creative ideas still have a place in the marketing strategy and are often the foundation of a successful campaign, that campaign can no longer survive without content to support it. In order to better understand Content Excellence, let's first break down what content is exactly.

Essentially, content is communication people choose to spend time with. This is not limited to advertisements or copy—content can be anything. Coca-Cola is a key brand that has embraced this change from creative excellence to Content Excellence. As explained

FIGURE 4–3   Content Excellence.

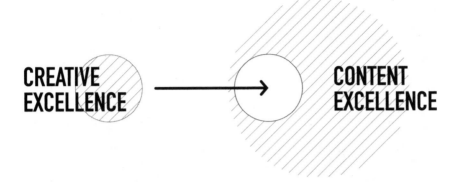

in the Coca-Cola 2020 video, Content Excellence is the vehicle through which dynamic stories are told. Coca-Cola defines dynamic stories as "the development of incremental elements of a brand idea that get dispersed systematically across multiple channels of conversation for the purpose of creating a unified and coordinated brand experience." In other words, Storyliving is a vital component of creating a successful Content Excellence campaign.[4]

In an attempt to embrace this new ideology, Coca-Cola recently came out with a new bottle design that delivers its message of sharing happiness. Vending machines were strategically placed on college campuses during freshman orientation and dispensed bottles that could only be opened when paired with another bottle. The idea was that not only would students get to enjoy their refreshing Coke, but they would get to do so with new friends. Coca-Cola released a video featuring the new bottles and the reactions from students and posted it to the Coca-Cola YouTube page. The video achieved instant popularity and was shared across networks.

This type of marketing could never have been imagined a decade ago. But now, with the emergence of content marketing, brands across the nation are creating similar interactive campaigns that encourage participation and generate energy around a product. Lowe's also embraced this idea of content marketing when it released its Fix in Six campaign that featured quick household tips in the six-second Vine format. According to the 2014 "Home Buyer and Seller Generational Trends" report published by the National Association of Realtors, Millennials with at least one child under the age of 18 constitute 23 percent of all homebuyers.[5] Millennial homeowners are also more likely than any other generation of homeowners to say that their next home will be a house they can fix up. This emphasizes the DIY and "fix-it" mentality of young adult homeowners—typically, those who are also beginning new families. Overall, there is a huge opportunity for home improvement brands to connect with these young parents, who are also more than likely first-time homeowners. Lowe's successfully attempted to connect with this demographic through its "Fix in Six" videos, which share advice such as: "Use walnuts to remove light scratches on wood. The oils will fill in the scratches! #lowesfxinsix." (We tried this—it really works!) When you consider who is using the Vine app, you find that there is an overwhelming Millennial presence. According to research conducted by ComScore, there is a 10.7 percent penetration rate of Vine by Millennials, ranking it as the seventh-most-used social media app among young adults between the ages of 18 and 34 with smartphones. How does this apply to Millennial parents? Simple: As Millennials themselves, these parents are the ones who are turning to the Lowe's Vine videos for quick home improvement tips.

The goal with Content Excellence is to challenge brands to think outside the box and go beyond traditional methods of advertis-ing and consumer engagement. Content Excellence is what in-spires relationships, and, as we have learned, relationships lead

IF THE CONTENT

created does not have a place in the lives of consumers, they will skip over it without a second thought and move on to another brand that offers content that does.

to happy, loyal customers. If the content created does not have a place in the lives of consumers, they will skip over it without a sec-ond thought and move on to another brand that offers content that does. In a Millennial-driven economy, content is the key to creating conversations and inviting Millennials in as cocreators and brand partners.

MINDDRIVE is a nonprofit organization built to "inspire stu-dents to learn, expand their vision of the future and have a posi-tive influence on urban workforce development."[6] With a focus on urban youth, one of the classes offered by the program is Automo-tive Design, which pairs students with mentors so that, as a team, they turn an old clunker into a shiny electric car, improving their math, engineering, and communication skills along the way.

To encourage greater consciousness with a wider reach, an inno-vative social media campaign was created. The campaign was built around a trip to Washington, D.C.: The kids in the program were going to take their newly converted 1967 Karmann Ghia to the capital in hopes of talking with lawmakers about education reform. With the idea of Content Excellence in mind, MINDDRIVE cre-ated a "social fuel" campaign, which turned social buzz into actual energy, or fuel, for the car. They incorporated a "plea video" that featured students involved in MINDDRIVE talking about some of the challenges they faced and how the program gave them purpose and direction. In the video, the students asked viewers to share their story by watching, liking, posting, and hashtagging what they saw. Here's where it gets especially clever: An algorithm was developed that converted every impression on social media into "fuel" for the car. With a goal of 71,040 social watts to make the trip, the car was fitted with a special device that received the social wattage and powered the car to move forward. If there was not enough social wattage for the car to make the next leg of the trip, the car would not start.

The campaign quickly went viral and caught the attention of local, national, and even international news outlets. In total, over 450 news outlets throughout the world reported on the Social Fuel campaign for MINDDRIVE. Racking up almost a half-billion impressions, the students could have made their trip seven times! Additionally, and most important, the campaign attracted the attention of numerous philanthropists, who are opening branches of MINDDRIVE in five major U.S. cities, as well as Sydney, Australia. Linda Buchner, MINDDRIVE president, says, "The trip has been a humbling experience . . . a success yes, but also something more. People are connecting to the students and craving a solution to the same issues that are in every city and rural town in America."[7]

Millennial parents especially respond to this type of campaign because, for them, education is more than just sitting in a classroom. Millennial parents were the first generation of students to experience high-quality technology in the classroom, and they want the same thing for their children. A study conducted by the Center for the Digital Future found that not even half (47 percent) of the Millennial parent population believe that educators are "adequately preparing [students] to use new technologies."[8] Programs like

MINDDRIVE are extremely successful at connecting with Millennial parents because these programs engage them and their children in an educational campaign that is focused on learning through interaction, engagement, and technology—not just through lectures and homework.

Aside from the message of the campaign, what was it that made this a huge success? Content, content, content. In the future, brands will embrace this type of marketing and begin to include interactive campaign models in their strategic planning instead of focusing on traditional creative excellence.

In order to successfully execute a content-driven campaign, a deep understanding of the audience and its generational traits is essential. As we mentioned, content is about reaching the right person, at the right place, at the right time. In order to do this, brands will need to embrace the power behind Big Data. Now, choosing a channel is not as simple as picking whether to air an advertisement on NBC, ABC, or CBS. This shotgun approach does not connect with Millennial consumers—especially the more pragmatic Millennial parent consumers, who are more selective about the media they interact with. David Erickson, an expert in marketing and strategic communications with an emphasis on Internet marketing, says, "Beyond the demographics, beyond the psychographics, get into the technographics of what types of technology the target audience is using and how they're using it. Additionally, and frequently overlooked, are generational aspects of those audiences and how their generation plays into their attitudes toward content, and their attitudes toward technology, or just how they react to certain messages."[9] When applying this insight to our analysis of Millennials and Millennial parents, it is clear that their use of technology is vastly different from that of any other generation. The 2014 BabyCenter report found that Millennial moms spend 8.3 hours online per week compared to the 7.4 hours per week Gen X moms spend online.[10]

As consumers are becoming more and more digitally native (children of Millennials have never even experienced life without tech simplicity and the Internet), content is beginning to live in the digital space as opposed to traditional marketing outlets. Plum Organics, one of the leading baby food brands among Millennial parents, is no stranger to creating content-driven campaigns that engage a new population of moms and dads. The company was founded in 2007 and has since become a top competitor when it comes to innovative baby food products. Not only do its products completely align with Millennial values—fresh ingredients, innovative packaging, and conscious capitalism—but the company also connects with Millennials in the digital space, creating campaigns that encourage the creation of user-generated content (UGC). UGC is a highly effective way to connect with Millennial Mindset consumers because it completely embraces the notion of cocreation.

In an effort to capitalize on this type of content strategy, Plum Organics created the Amazing Moments campaign in 2013. The campaign encouraged Millennial parents to share their baby's "amazing moments." Digital native moms could not wait to post their favorite moments to the Plum Organics social media pages. Parents posted videos of their little one's first steps, giggles, and words. The best pictures and videos were used to create a two-minute spot that aired on the Plum Organics YouTube channel and was shared almost instantly. We watched the video (you know, for research purposes), and we must say that it's hard to watch the video without smiling. The overall campaign garnered more than 12 million impressions and hundreds of video submissions. Additionally, out of the hundreds of videos that were submitted, 70 percent of consumers who entered the contest opted in to the Plum database. This campaign did exceptionally well within the Millennial demographic because it touched on key Millennial trends: cocreation, sharing, and purpose-driven content.

According to the BabyCenter study, Millennial moms are 20 percent more likely to take/share videos online than their Gen X counterparts. This is due in large part to their ability to learn to navigate technology at a quicker rate. They are more knowledgeable about online privacy settings and can easily adjust who can view their pictures and media pages. The same BabyCenter report found that Millennial moms do not settle for Facebook's default privacy settings and will turn off location services when the option is available. With these advancements in privacy technology, content that encourages photo sharing has become increasingly popular—especially with Millennial moms who seek out opportunities to share pictures and videos of their little pride and joy.

Traditionally, brand communications all led to a call to action, which in most cases was a sales pitch. With Plum Organics, the call to action was less about a sale and more about an interaction. Remember when we told you to forget the AIDA model? This is another great example of how the Brand Atom is more relevant to the Millennial Mindset customer. As a result of this new type of communication, the success metric was not necessarily based on the number of conversions but, rather, on the impact on loyalty and relationships. This is the underlying key to creating a successful content campaign. The sale cannot be the call to action because Millennials will not buy into it. They want to interact, have a conversation, and get engaged. Only then will they *think* about making a purchase or donation.

The Content Excellence Landscape

When it comes to content, there is no single format that works best when engaging Millennial Mindset consumers. Inspired by the Altimeter Group, FutureCast developed a content matrix that can be utilized when developing a content strategy (see Figure 4–4). The matrix is divided into planned and unplanned content and proactive and reactive content. The X axis is consumer based—brands are responding to consumer engagement—whereas the Y axis is based on the brands' ability to control or plan for a situation. Based on this matrix, we can divide content type into four distinct quadrants: Branded Content, Rooted Content, Social Care, and Social Satellite. Each quadrant correlates with specific content strategies that brands can use to engage their brand partners.

Rooted Content

Traditionally, brands focused on the Rooted Content area, in the top right quadrant of the matrix. These brand interactions are both planned and proactive and can be developed over a long period of time. Rooted content is essentially promotional and anticipated events like product launches and general public relations campaigns. Corporate sponsorships also often fall into this category because they are both planned and proactive. Sponsorships allow

FIGURE 4–4 Content matrix.

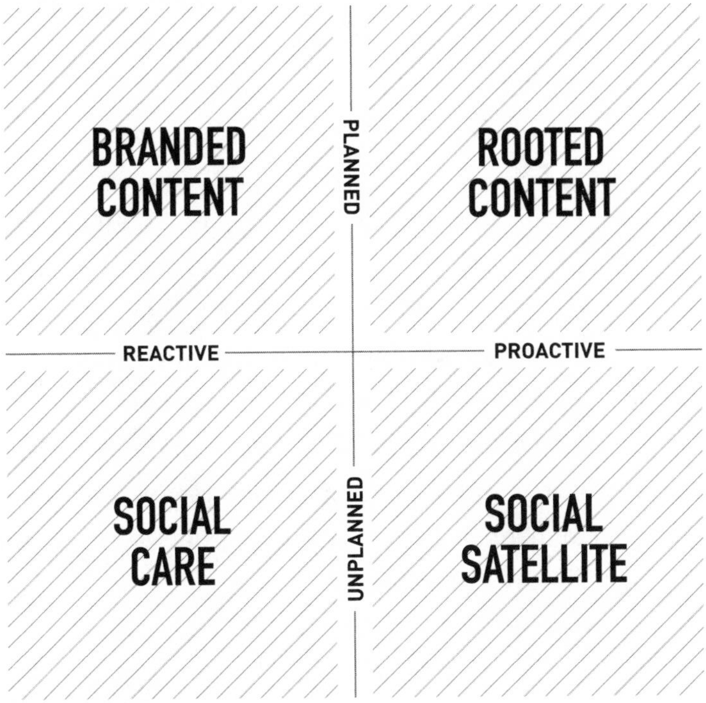

brands to align themselves with popular events that garner a large and engaged audience. Remember that adorable Vicks VapoRub commercial featuring Drew Brees, the New Orleans Saints quarterback, and his son? Vicks is an official NFL sponsor, and the commercial aired during the games when viewership was at its peak. The advertisement resonated with the Millennial dads who were tuning in for the game. The emotional appeal of the ad in addition to its alignment with one of the most watched sporting programs of the year—particularly among the male demographic—scored it a top rank on the list of most watched advertisements by Millennial dads.

After the advertisement aired, *Fortune* magazine referred to Brees as a "golden-goose image as an endorser of wholesome, family products." Brees said in an interview for the magazine that representing family products for men is 100 percent his focus.[11]

Social Care

Social Care is another piece of the social content strategy we have seen more recently popping up all over social media. This is the one-on-one interaction brands have with their consumers. Social Care is the content brands curate when they engage in daily customer service, or address a problem, or want to build stronger loyalty among individual customers. Typically, a brand is reacting to an issue or current event and has not planned a response. Honey Maid made quite a statement in 2014 when responding to backlash from its Wholesome Family campaign.

It all started on March 11, 2014. Honey Maid released an advertisement as part of its Wholesome Family campaign that focused on the inclusivity of the "modern" family. The ad featured real Millennial families in all their diverse glory, including gay, interracial, and stereotypical rocker families. The "controversial" advertisement (which brought us to tears) received mixed reviews. In an effort to combat the negative responses the ad received and praise those who spoke highly of the TV spot, Honey Maid released a follow-up video just a few weeks later, which was posted to its YouTube page. The video featured two artists using rolled-up, printed copies of every comment posted about the original ad and placing them in a pattern that spelled the word "love." The video highlighted the fact that there were nearly 10 times as many positive comments as negative comments. Honey Maid's very classy response to the criticism of the original ad scored it big points with Millennials who believe in a new family model. The brand was not able to plan for the responses the ad would get but swiftly worked to put together a response that resonated with each individual customer who contributed to the conversation.

Branded Content

Branded Content is the type of tailored content that typically comes to mind when discussing Content Excellence. It is both planned and reactive in that brands have the capability to plan for an event, like the Super Bowl or the Academy Awards ceremony, but react based on who the winners are or what happens during the actual event. For example, during the 2014 Academy Awards ceremony, Ellen DeGeneres famously took the most retweeted selfie of all time. (Come on, we know you retweeted it, too.) The scripted selfie involved Ellen using her Samsung Galaxy, a move that Samsung had actively planned for. What it did not plan for, however, was the high response rate of fans. Samsung was able to leverage that publicity to generate more awareness and sales. Branded Content is also commonly found in many user-generated content campaigns. Brands have the capability of planning for a campaign that encourages customers to share their experiences, pictures, or videos, but then they must react to the submissions they receive. Starbucks is one of the leading brands when it comes to UGC. Don't believe us? Log in to Instagram and search #Starbucks. A majority of the entries won't be from the company but from satisfied Millennial customers.

Social Satellite

Successful brands have implemented what we like to call a Social Satellite, also commonly referred to as the Brand Newsroom. In the same way a satellite orbits the galaxy, collecting data that can be used to predict future events, a Social Satellite is a team that monitors social media in real time in order to stay up-to-date on trends, create immediate interactions with consumers, and be proactive in regard to brand promotion. These interactions are both unplanned and proactive. Sound confusing? We'll explain.

Think about your elevator pitch. What is the purpose of that speech? You have it prepared so that you can be proactive when you meet a new client in an unplanned setting. It is both proactive and unplanned. Brands that incorporate Social Satellites are essentially preparing their elevator pitches. They are using their resources to create real-time content that is proactive, but they do not know what that content will be used for yet. The goal is to utilize resources in order to find opportunities for a brand in environments where it is not currently communicating. Whereas it is important for social managers to monitor conversations and look for real-time engagement opportunities, it is more critical that they look beyond current conversations to find new opportunities to create dialogue—within the brand authority, of course. Social Satellites are still a relatively new concept in the marketing industry, and brands are still determining the right way to incorporate them into the internal company structure.

In 2011, Luvs introduced its Heavy Duty Blowout Protection campaign. The commercials strayed from showing the traditional blue liquid that had always been used to display the durable qualities of the diaper and instead featured an *American Idol*–style game show in which animated toddlers were judged on their "blowouts" to the tune of "Poop! There It Is!" The humor used in the ad engaged Millennial parents and took a new approach to the functionalistic aspects of the diaper. Let's face it—unscented blue liquid isn't coming out of anyone's baby. As a part of the campaign, Luvs created the Heavy Dooty Blowout Challenge. The challenge encouraged young parents to go online to the Luvs Facebook challenge page and click the "Drop a Dooty" button. Every time someone clicked the button, not only would Luvs donate diapers to Project Night Night (a nonprofit organization that works with families in need of basic necessities) but also the diaper of a gigantic, 20-foot-tall inflatable baby at the Mall of America would get bigger.

Sound gross? A little bit. But the real-time engagement was a huge win with Millennial parents. Anyone visiting the Mall of America was able to see the real-time response, as the baby's diaper continued to fill with "dooty" throughout the duration of the challenge. The Facebook page also featured a real-time video feed and a counter tallying the number of diapers being donated. At the end of the campaign, a total of 60,000 Luvs diapers were donated and the online conversation surrounding Luvs increased exponentially. The key in this campaign was the real-time interactions that were happening between Luvs customers and the brand itself. Essentially, the campaign created a Social Satellite that allowed Luvs to monitor social media 24/7 and generate real-time relationships and communications with customers in an authentic and transparent way.

One big "aha" from this matrix is the idea that the content landscape requires *much* more listening than brand marketers are engaging in today. When discussing content strategy, the conversation almost always shifts to the volume or quantity of content that brands are able to push out. However, shoving out branded content should not be the intention in today's marketing strategy. The intention is to use this matrix to reach the right people at the right time, when they are excited to communicate with the brand. Traditionally, brands were focused more on the top half of the matrix, on Branded Content and Rooted Content. These two quadrants rely heavily on talking to consumers. They are events or promotional campaigns that have been strategically planned with the right message and overall intent. However, the golden nugget lies within the bottom half of the matrix, in the Social Care and Social Satellite quadrants, which rely more on listening to consumers and responding to what is already engaging them in the social space. As we can see in Figure 4–5, the traditional flow went from the top half down; the Branded Content and Rooted Content influenced what consumers were saying about a brand. Now, however, it is the prosumers who are influencing the type of planned and promotional events brands are creating.

As we step into the future of marketing, brands that win will accept this new message development strategy and begin focusing on content as opposed to just the idea itself. Especially when considering Millennial parents, it is essential to create content that they

FIGURE 4–5   Content flow.

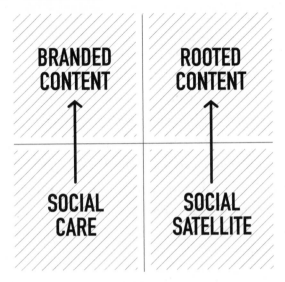

NEW MODEL

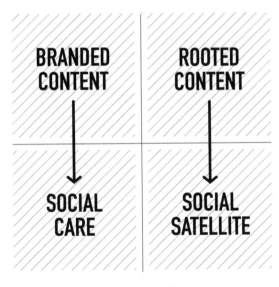

OLD MODEL

can participate in because they believe in a new model of partnership even beyond that espoused by nonparent Millennial consumers. Millennial parents are redefining what partnership means in regard to parenting, but, more important for you, dear reader, in regard to brand partnerships. For example, Millennial moms prefer content that is playful, honest, and authentic and are more likely to interact with brands that do not just align with these values but give them something that *incorporates* these values in ways that they can *interact* with. The brands that successfully implement this type of content will be more likely to develop partnerships and drive action. The importance of content is not a Millennial creation, but it is heightened by the interaction Millennials expect to have with any brand.

CHAPTER 4: KEY TAKEAWAYS

- ⮌ **Fuhgeddaboudit.** As Johnny Depp's character in the 1997 hit movie *Donnie Brasco* said, "Forget about it." It's time to put the old models of marketing in a box and toss it out. Millennials are changing the game when it comes to connecting with customers. They value two-way communication over one-way conversations, engagement over segmentation, and inclusion over exclusion. These changes are reflected in the transition from the AIDA model to the Brand Atom model, which focuses more on partnership, intrigue, meaning, and energy.

- ⮌ **Content is the new creative.** Creative ideas and strategy are not enough for brands engaging the Millennial generation. Now it is all about engagement and campaigns that foster interaction and crowdsourcing. Content is the type of communication people choose to spend time with, and more and more Millennials are choosing to spend time with brands that embrace a content-driven campaign. In order to successfully activate this type of campaign, brands must incorporate all pieces of the content strategy matrix: Branded Content, Rooted Content, Social Care, and Social Satellite.

- ⮌ **The roles have switched.** Traditionally, Branded Content influenced the way consumers perceived a brand. Now the roles have switched, and it is the consumer who is affecting the messages each brand creates. The era of user-generated content and Social Satellites has led to a new marketing infrastructure that is determined by the way consumers are interacting with the brand, not the way the brand is interacting with the consumer.

CHAPTER 5

The Middle of the Road Could Be the End

It's not surprising that, generally speaking, parents have to stretch their dollars further than they did when there were fewer mouths to feed. Many Millennials are reaching their peak spending years after graduating from college and beginning their careers; however, student loan debt, underemployment, and lack of available jobs are weighing on them as they begin the next chapter of their lives. Analysis of a 2012 national financial capability study shows that 55 percent of the 25,000 Millennial study participants currently have outstanding student loan debt and about half are concerned about their ability to pay it off.[1]

Millennials graduating from college have been seriously affected by the Great Recession of 2008 and have since felt the sting of underemployment.[2] Their higher rate of underemployment has added fuel to the start-up nation fire. The number of Millennials who aspire to own their own businesses and who are using their resources to make their own jobs as opposed to entering the faltering workforce has increased exponentially. Additionally, as Millennials start their own families, the need for budgeting and financial planning has caused them to rearrange many of the priorities they had before having children. Parties and entertainment are taking a backseat to appliances and groceries. Time to get responsible!

Robin, a married mom, quit her job as a program coordinator for a healthcare IT company when her now 2-year-old daughter was born, which shifted her family's financial priorities quickly. Before, they would buy what they wanted to buy, when they wanted it, with very little planning or forethought. "We have to think about the future now, things like college funds. We were at the store today thinking about the next car seat we have to buy, so we're going to start saving up for that."

Price Is King, Convenience Is Queen

The FutureCast "Millennials as New Parents Study" asked parents of this generation how they spent money before starting a family compared to how they spend it now. Participants were given ten categories and asked to indicate, on a sliding scale, whether they were more likely to purchase a product based on price or quality. If they made a decision completely based on quality, they were told to select 100 as their answer. Likewise, if they purchased it based completely on price, they were told to select 0 as their answer. In eight of the ten spending categories tested, there was a significant shift from quality to price once they became parents.³ Figure 5–1 illustrates the shift from purchasing products based on quality (a score of 100 percent) as opposed to price (a score of 0 percent). This is a result of the pragmatism that is redefining the way Millennials are

---

FIGURE 5–1   Millennial parent spending, price vs. quality.

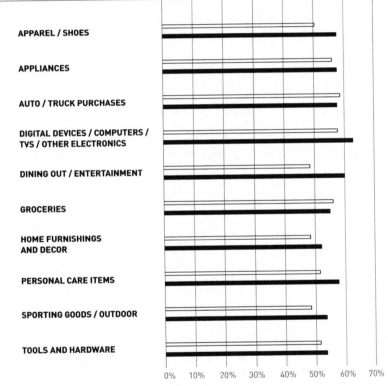

Source: David Gutting and Jeff Fromm, "Millennials as New Parents: The Rise of a New American Pragmatism," Barkley/FutureCast and Consumer Orbit research study, 2013.

approaching parenthood. Especially for parents in the Under Stress and Image First orbits, those making less than $45,000 a year, price trumps quality. However, they still expect brands to meet their high quality expectations. Pragmatism does not negate the high ideals Millennials held before having children; instead, it focuses on how to make those ideals a reality.

Before having children, one in six respondents was significantly more likely to make a purchase decision based on quality, rather than price, for dining and entertainment. After becoming parents, that number drops to only one in eleven. We can extrapolate that Millennial parents are more interested in finding family entertainment for more affordable prices and splurging on the products like groceries and appliances that affect the well-being of their children. Essentially, any product that has a direct impact on the child is still purchased based on quality over price.

Brand loyalty also plays an important role for Millennial parents. One of the greatest myths about Millennials is that they are not loyal to any brand and are constantly seeking out the best deals. Although discounts and coupons tend to sway Millennials (who doesn't love a good deal, right?), they tend be brand loyal when purchasing a product based on quality. However, Millennial moms reserve the right to cheat on their brands based on strong peer recommendations.

Even though price is a priority, convenience is not far behind, particularly when price differences aren't material. Millennials are always pegged as the "it's all about me" generation—something not so clearly borne out in research but in part derived from their rapid adoption of digital, social, and mobile technology—and let's not forget that this generation has basically invented the selfie.

Essentially, Millennials can expect to get whatever they want, whenever they want it. Although research has shown that they are far from selfish when it comes to cause marketing and values, they have grown up in an age when information is readily available and almost anything can be purchased immediately. Convenience is one of the driving forces that pushes a Millennial to purchase a product.

> Javina, mom to 2- and 4-year old boys, wants convenience in every aspect of the word. "I will try and get everything in one place but if I know that it's going to be a better deal, I'll make another trip. Just today, I went to Price Chopper [now Market 32] and Walmart because I knew that I could get body wash and soaps at a better price at Walmart, and I could get the rest of my groceries at Price Chopper. Price is also a factor for me. I look for the best specials and I'll shop where that is and if there are coupons, I'll definitely use those."

Even more convenient than physical distance from car to store is the ability to shop and make purchases on the couch, in front of the TV. Millennial parents—Millennial moms, in particular—use their smartphones for *everything*. Most moms will tell you that their smartphones are never more than an arm's length away because they are constantly checking their Facebook pages, often connecting with friends and family, and consulting parenting sites for new tips and products. In fact, research shows that Millennial moms spend an average of almost two hours a day on their smartphones, and Facebook is one of the their most used apps.[4] As digital natives, Millennials are constantly connected to each other and to brands via a variety of social networks. This constant connectivity has created an environment that enables a Millennial mom to do everything she needs to on her mobile phone or tablet from any place and at any time. The convenience factor plays a huge role for on-the-go parents who are seeking instant solutions to any problem or situation.

The increase in the amount of online shopping is also a result of the convenience factor desired by Millennials. Stephanie is a Millennial who spoke to us about her favorite shopping trends. "I love online shopping. It's addicting. I browse my favorite online stores weekly but my purchases are about monthly," Stephanie said. When we asked her about her latest purchase, she told us that she had just bought something online from Forever 21. This is perfectly aligned with FutureCast's original research about Millennial shopping trends, where survey participants were asked how much they agreed or disagreed with the statement "The convenience of online shopping is very important to me." Nearly 70 percent of all Millennial participants agreed with the statement, whereas less than 60 percent of non-Millennials agreed.[5] Now Millennials are using their smartphones to research products before they buy them. Gone are the days of spending hours in Best Buy trying to find the best deal on that new must-have gadget. This change in the shopping environment has also affected the way new parents are purchasing products digitally. Research from the BabyCenter report shows that 44 percent of Millennial moms have made a purchase on their smartphone in the previous week.[6] As a marketer, it is important to utilize mobile and digital platforms when working with your Millennial partners. If their needs for convenience and differentiation are not met . . . prepare for divorce.

Monkey in the Middle

Now that we have explored price, quality, and convenience through the Millennial perspective, the question that arises is this: How do these factors impact the type of consumers Millennials are becoming and the effect they are having on multiunit retail/restaurant, consumer packaged goods (CPG), and consumer marketers? (After all, that is one of the reasons why you're reading this book, right?) It's simple—Millennials are drawn to the extremes. We see Millennials flocking to the quality of high-end stores or the convenience of discount stores with little room for midrange companies to grow and thrive. The era of high-low budgeting is upon us, leaving those in the middle of the road with increased competition from both ends of the spectrum. According to a survey conducted among 1,200 Millennials by Ypulse, 51 percent of respondents said they are willing to splurge on a luxury item if they buy inexpensive products elsewhere in order to balance out their budget.[7]

In order to better understand the impact of high-low budgeting, let's explore how this change is affecting the grocery industry. At the top end of the grocery industry are stores like Whole Foods, which are leading the pack when it comes to high-quality, local, and organic products. However, with higher quality comes a higher price. Millennials are no longer those ramen noodle–eating college students they once were and are now more interested in food that not only tastes good but also comes from an authentic source. They are also preparing more meals for themselves at home and hosting dinner parties for their friends that do not feature red Solo cups and the cheapest beer at the store. In fact, Millennials are leading the clean-eating health food kick that has taken over the food industry. The "Millennials as New Parents" study found that more than two in five Millennial parents support the "local food movement"; look for foods fortified with more protein, fiber, and antioxidants; look for food with fewer artificial ingredients; and buy organic food whenever they can.[8]

Millennials are often more aware of the authenticity of the food they are eating than other generations have been. They want to know where it came from, how it was produced, and who made it, posing a challenge for more traditional, regional supermarket chains. Figure 5–2 accurately portrays the growing Millennial sentiment about food consciousness and how Millennials are more concerned with what they are putting in their bodies than with what they look like.

Trader Joe's has successfully tapped into the Millennial parent market by guaranteeing that its products contain no artificial flavors, artificial colors, preservatives, MSG, genetically modified ingredients, or trans fats. Trader Joe's has positioned itself as the "neighborhood grocery store." Founded in 1957, Trader Joe's has changed the grocery game when it comes to quality-driven store brands. The company website boasts that at Trader Joe's "you won't find a lot of branded items." This means that Trader Joe's is putting a private label brand on a higher pedestal than big corporate brands. This will ultimately create a significant shift in the business models of other major grocery retailers.

There is no question why many Millennials favor Trader Joe's over some more traditional grocery store chains. Research shows that Millennials are more concerned with the authenticity of their food products than other generations. Why do you think Millennials are willing to pay so much for a burrito at Chipotle? Trader Joe's

FIGURE 5–2 Millennial parent nutrition and health perceptions.

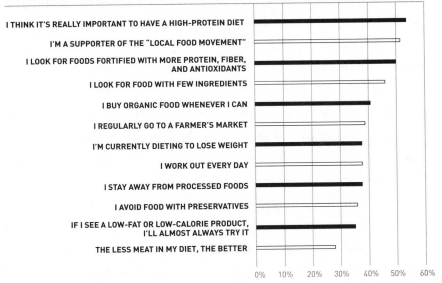

HOW STRONGLY DO YOU AGREE OR DISAGREE WITH EACH OF THE FOLLOWING STATEMENTS ON NUTRITION AND HEALTH?

Source: David Gutting and Jeff Fromm, "Millennials as New Parents: The Rise of a New American Pragmatism," Barkley/FutureCast and Consumer Orbit research study, 2013.

has capitalized on the health kick among Millennials and created a business platform that is essentially driven by the Millennial Mindset consumer. The Millennial Mindset consumer is a new breed of shopper who is not a Millennial by definition but has adopted the Millennial Mindset when it comes to purchase patterns and decisions. For example, many Gen Xers are jumping on board with the health trend and are eating in a way that is very similar to the way Millennials eat. This has led not only to an increased presence of Millennial shoppers at retailers like Trader Joe's but also to an increase in the Millennial Mindset among consumers who are not part of the Millennial generation. Although there is a relatively low level of social media presence for Trader Joe's, it has successfully created a mom-and-pop environment that is perfect for shoppers looking to "go local."

Millennial food trends have changed the direction of home cooking. Millennials overwhelmingly have more desire to cook with exotic foods using recipes that allow them to be creative in the kitchen. This means that Millennials are willing to shop at multiple retailers in order to find all of the ingredients necessary to prepare their dream dishes. This also means that stores no longer have a captive audience—just because shoppers are there to buy groceries doesn't mean they will buy every item at that store.

In Figure 5–3 we can see how Millennials are interacting with brands based on where they fall on the Love Curve provided by BERA Brand Management. Trader Joe's does well with Millennials because they are able to offer high-quality products that instill confidence in the shopper, all at a reasonable price. It has also built a brand that is differentiated and purposeful to Millennial parents, leveraging the brand love model we discussed in Chapter 3. Trader Joe's continues to be fresh and new and has a lock on that sweet spot between dating and love that every company wants to hit. Not to mention that the smoothies at Trader Joe's are always a bonus. (Be sure to try the strawberry chia smoothie—you won't regret it.)

Whole Foods is another example of a high-end grocery store that connects strongly with the Millennial parent, but in a different way than Trader Joe's. While Trader Joe's creates a mom-and-pop feel, Whole Foods has positioned itself as a leader in the organic

FIGURE 5–3 Millennial parent grocery Love Curve.

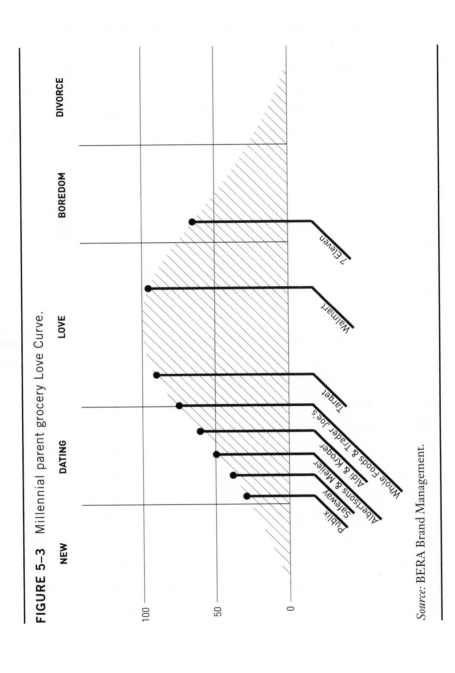

Source: BERA Brand Management.

food space. Unlike Trader Joe's, Whole Foods has a strong digital strategy and presence, ranking number two on *Fortune's* list of social media superstars in 2014. By leveraging its more than 525 local social media accounts, Whole Foods can have a personal connection with its communities and shoppers, with employees trained to answer queries at a local level.[9] Its digital strategy also includes education, with a social media program in 2013 that aimed to teach shoppers about genetically modified organisms (GMOs) using social media to answer questions and engage customers in discussion when it announced in early 2013 that it would begin labeling GMOs.

Being in the middle of the road in the grocery industry has become increasingly fraught with challenges. Even with 1,335 and 1,075 stores, respectively, both Safeway and Albertsons have struggled to thrive and grow in this economy. In early 2014, a merger of the two large chains was announced, which will allow the resulting mega-chain to remain competitive in the ever-divergent grocery industry. Proponents of the merger argue that by combining forces Albertsons and Safeway will be able to offer lower prices and better-quality food products. Millennial parents are very cost driven when it comes to grocery shopping but are not willing to compromise the quality of the food they are purchasing. FutureCast's research found that close to 40 percent of Millennials with children who participated in the survey want to take advantage of a manufacturer's discount or special offer compared to only a little more than 20 percent of Millennials who are not yet parents.[10] This could prove to be beneficial for the Safeway-Albertsons merger, as they aim to appeal to both the price and quality desires of Millennials.

Regional grocers are getting more creative about finding ways to cater not only to the Millennial mom but also to the Millennial

Mindset in general. John Yerkes has been in the grocery business most of his adult life. He has worked in, and ultimately helped run, his parents' small chain of regional grocery stores until just recently, when they sold the chain and drove into the sunset of retirement. Why didn't John just take over those stores when his parents retired? "I saw traditional [grocery] stores as a more and more difficult business model to run. They are being hit from so many angles, from Trader Joe's to Whole Foods to dollar stores, convenience stores, online. They are big and they are expensive." With a deep understanding of grocery operations, and having watched shoppers change significantly over the past two decades, John had a better idea. That is how Zoomin Market was born.

Zoomin market is a drive-through grocery store, modeled after the successful drive-through chains in Europe, particularly Chronodrive in France. Zoomin Market shoppers go online, select the items they want by brand name or product type or by browsing the virtual aisles, check out, select a pickup time, then zoom in and pick up their bags full of groceries. Is the United States ready for this? Yerkes thinks so, but understands the challenges. "Our biggest hurdle is changing habits. We are not just competing against other grocery stores. We are competing with convenience."

This "order online" model aligns with the Millennial mom in many ways. First, there is the convenience factor—have you ever taken two young children into a grocery store and down the cereal aisle? With Zoomin, Mom does all of her product selection online and can pick up the groceries without having to get out of the car, or, better yet, she can send her husband to pick up the groceries (with no chance that he'll mess it up).

Having opened the doors in spring 2014, Zoomin Market is still new and is working out the kinks as it learns from customers. Customer feedback is an important part of the process in order to understand what is working, what isn't, and what needs to be improved. But it's not just the customers who are participating in this brand journey; it's the employees, too. When hiring, John didn't require a college degree but, rather, a sense of creativity and excitement about this concept. He says, "We really had fun with the interviews. The concept itself brought people out who were excited about something new and innovative."

With his new staff of mostly Millennials, John found himself in the conundrum that many business owners face: a delay in the building and operations. He had already hired employees with a promised start date, so, instead of waiting around for the doors to open, he put their skills to use. For the three months between the time he hired his staff and when the store finally opened, these Millennial employees came up with new systems and improvements to the process, social media ideas, and marketing content. "It was a real blessing and surprise because they took it upon themselves to help build this business. They felt like 'I want to be part of this team.'" John found that it is not only Millennial consumers who want to cocreate to build a brand; employees do, too. Involving stakeholders in the cocreation process, from customers to staff to management, can lead to a more holistic brand. Not to mention, of course, that happy employees often lead to happy customers.

While many middle-of-the-road stores are losing ground with Millennial parents, discount stores such as Walmart have remained unaffected or have even experienced growth. In fact, in a recent FutureCast study, which asked Millennials to make a list of their top ten brands, Walmart ranked number ten for Millennials who are not parents and jumped up to the number four spot for Millennial parents.[11] Why is the not-particularly-hip store so popular among Millennials, especially Millennial parents? Contrary to popular belief, it isn't always about the "coolest" brand (or in this case, maybe the "least uncool" brand), but, rather, it comes back to the king and queen of shopping priorities for Millennial parents—price and convenience—both of which Walmart consistently delivers on. Even within the mass retailer space, some might think that Millennials would prefer the Target experience over Walmart, but in the same research, when Millennials were asked which store they would choose if they could shop at only one store for the rest of their lives, Walmart consistently won out over Target. While both stores offer convenience, Walmart has established itself as a low-cost leader.

Additionally, Walmart has mastered the art of high-low budgeting. Walmart understands that Millennials are going to spend money on products that are beyond their budget. A 2012 study found that, on average, Millennial college students spend $784 per month on discretionary expenses.[12] However, they plan to make up for that spending by saving pennies elsewhere. Enter Walmart—the ultimate retailer for a budget-conscious shopper. The "Everyday Low Price" model created by Walmart has won over the masses of Millennial shoppers by guaranteeing the lowest prices all year round and offering to price-match any other retail provider. Millennial parents also highly value the convenience of Walmart as the catchall retailer. Need an inexpensive new pair of shoes for your child? Get it at Walmart. Going on a family vacation and want to grab some cheap beach toys? Get them at Walmart. And while you're there, why not get all of your groceries as well? Oh, and don't forget that six-pack of your favorite beer. Millennials with children are also more likely than their nonparent counterparts to shop in bulk in order to stock up rather than purchasing individual products for themselves or at the last minute. Walmart is the ideal retailer for bulk shopping (unless we also consider club membership retailers like Sam's Club and Costco) that provides essentially everything new Millennial parents need for their households.

What about retail industries besides grocery? The same high-low trend exists, with middle-of-the-road retailers going out of business or combining forces to create an oligopoly that includes one or two large-format retailers. Plus, the emergence of e-commerce retailers has changed the retail game. The consumer electronics industry is a great example. What used to be a fairly crowded market has dwindled for the most part to two main players: Best Buy and Amazon. The same trend exists with office stores. Office Depot and Office Max started a merger in November 2013, putting them in competition with Staples and, well, Amazon. Have you noticed that Amazon keeps coming up?

As we have seen, Millennials and Millennial parents are concerned with getting the most bang for their buck. They are doing their research online before making large-scale purchases and are seeking out discounts and coupons that can be used to cut costs. Amazon is a site that combines both of these key Millennial values and is consistently innovating and growing with the up-and-coming demographic. Like Walmart, Amazon has successfully tapped into cost and convenience, but has done so in a way that is incredibly relevant to the Millennial Mindset. Millennials can compare prod-

WHY IS AMAZON KILLING IT WITH MILLENNIALS?

1. Convenient
2. Price comparison
3. Reviews/recommendations
4. Constant innovation (come on, drones?!)
5. Unique, highly useful brand

---

ucts and prices and search for the exact product they are looking for, then have it delivered directly to their door. Amazon has also created an environment in which people don't go to shop—they go to buy. One might argue that there is a loss of impulse opportunity when your customers are only buying and not shopping, but Amazon combats that with a sophisticated recommendation system (how do they always know what I need before I need it?), as well as suggestions for items that enhance or work with the product already in the shopping cart. (See sidebar, above.) Similar to the Netflix recommendation system, this method is successful with Millennials because it's providing exactly what they want, when they want it (and sometimes even before they know they want it).

According to the "Millennials as New Parents" research conducted by FutureCast, Amazon was ranked one of the top ten brands for Millennial parents. Additionally, when asked where they have made a purchase during the past month, roughly 65 percent of Millennial parents mentioned Amazon.[13] This comes as no surprise, as online shopping is becoming more prevalent among new mothers. Sites like Amazon can be accessed from ultimately any platform (desktop, mobile, tablet, etc.) and are updated based on real-time purchases. Additionally, Amazon's Subscribe and Save services for top brands for Millennial parents (Pampers, Huggies, and Gerber, to name a few) allows moms to have diapers and baby food delivered to the door before they run out. For Millennial parents specifically, the convenience offered by e-commerce shopping make it a more viable option for household shopping. This brings us back to how important pragmatism is in connecting with Millennial parents. When it comes to high-low budgeting, Millennials look for outlets that allow them to get the most bang for the buck, and Amazon has certainly established its authority as the go-to retailer for high-quality products, at an affordable price, that is convenient for shoppers.

Convenience Isn't Always Convenient

Here's the thing about convenience: It can't just be easier *in theory*; it has to be convenient *in practice*, too. Self-checkouts in grocery stores are one of the best examples of this disconnect between theory and practice. Imagine this: You're at the grocery store to get baby formula and a candy bar (to stress-eat on the car ride home, of course), so waiting in line behind the woman with two cartloads full of groceries, a handful of coupons, and a checkbook buried at the bottom of her purse is too much to handle. Giving shoppers the option to check themselves out without having to stand behind this woman, or having to interact with other human beings, is great on paper. But in practice, self-checkouts haven't delivered.

Self-checkout has been around for more than fifteen years. The Food Marketing Institute reported that only 6 percent of U.S. supermarkets offered self-checkout lanes in 1999, and by 2007 only 5 percent of stores *didn't* have them.[14] While most of the nation is turning to automated commerce devices (the Sprinkles Cupcake ATM is the first thing that comes to mind), self-checkout at grocery stores is not cutting it when it comes to robotic commerce convenience. Why is this? Self-checkouts actually require more work for the customer. In the published report "Dancing with Robots," economist Frank Levy explains that, in order for a computerized system to substitute for human work the program must meet two conditions:

1. All information necessary to carry out the task must be written in a way that can be understood by computers.
2. The job must have a consistent routine that can be explained in rules.[15]

Self-checkouts clearly meet the second condition. You scan the item, put it in your bag, and pay—a simple process. However, the first condition is the one that most computerized checkout systems can't handle. A human can tell the difference between a sweet potato and a regular potato, but the information takes much longer to type into a computerized system, especially when the person operating the machine is unfamiliar with the codes required to make the computer process the information. For Millennial parents, the theory of self-checkout is a good one—who wouldn't want to get in and out of the grocery store as quickly as possible when shopping with children? In reality, what parent wants to deal with the issues that present themselves as a result of self-checkout systems? Parents typically choose traditional checkout lanes when shopping. Kristy, mom to an 11-year old son, says, "Sometimes the machine tells you 'items not in bag,' or it won't ring it up right. There are certain things that you really can't do with self-checkout. It's kind of a pain, so I avoid them. Sometimes it's longer than just waiting in line." As a result of these challenges, many grocery chains are beginning to remove their self-checkout machines altogether. Big Y, the Springfield, Massachusetts–based grocery store, pulled self-checkout machines back in 2011, claiming that the machines did not fulfill the standard the company wanted to set regarding customer service. Kroger soon followed suit, and many other chains are considering dumping the self-checkout systems as well.[16]

There are many ways, however, in which the right technology can boost convenience, especially for Millennial parents. Look no further than Zulily. Cofounded in 2009 by Darrell Cavens along with Mark Vadon, founder of the successful jewelry website Blue Nile, Zulily managed to turn a profit and go public in three short years.[17] This daily deal site has had its fair share of competition, including Groupon, Gilt, Rue La La, and Fab. Fortunately, Zulily managed to differentiate itself in this market and appeal to a specific target: Millennial moms looking for deals.

How'd the company do it? It provided deals it knew Millennial moms could not resist: coupons offering up to 70 percent off of baby and children's products. This tactic accurately portrays how companies are adapting to the new price-over-quality desire on the part of Millennial parents. The shift from quality to price doesn't necessarily mean that quality or image-conscious brands are no longer desirable; it just means that a low price often trumps those qualities. Think about what parents buy for their children: diapers, clothes, shoes, even furniture for the home that can withstand the wrath of toddlers. Value has a different meaning when the life span of a product is limited.

Zulily gives moms the opportunity to buy the quality items they want, such as boutique clothing for their children at deeply

WHAT IS GAMIFICATION?

Gamification is a marketing strategy that uses typical elements of a game (point scoring, competition, etc.) in order to boost consumer engagement. These interactive platforms are highly successful when it comes to marketing to Millennials because they create an exciting environment that differentiates one brand from another. According to Gabe Zichermann, founder of Gamification Co., intrinsic reinforcement, dopamine priming, and the winner effect work together to change a Millennial's motivations when interacting with a brand that incorporates gamification into its marketing strategy.

discounted prices. But, wait, there's more! The limited-time flash sale environment gamifies the shopping experience (see "What Is Gamification"). Zulily e-mails registered members every morning at six o'clock to tell them what products are being offered and what the discounted prices will be. The catch is that the flash sale lasts only seventy-two hours, so you better get moving! Items also usually sell out quickly—and when they are gone, they are gone for good. Receiving the daily e-mails and checking the Zulily app for the newest deals is a form of entertainment for Millennial moms as much as it is a shopping experience. Customer responses on the site are extremely positive. One user even said, "My phone is within arm's reach and it's one of the first things I do. News and email and Zulily."[18] Additionally, Zulily says that the products themselves come from boutique retailers and emerging brands that otherwise would be hard to find. That gives vendors an audience of millions and customers the sense of discovering new things.[19]

Other deal websites have struggled to create repeat business after the coupon is used, which is an inherent flaw in the business model. Cavens notes that with Zulily this is not an issue because repeat purchasing of babies' and children's products is different from that for all other types of merchandise. Parents often fall in love with a specific brand, returning for repeat orders of other gear or recommending the items to friends.[20] As we have seen, Millennial moms are prone to making and following peer recommendations and are loyal to brands that have the quality they prefer at the prices they are comfortable with—not to mention that the convenience of having everything you order shipped directly to your door comes in handy for a new mom who needs to balance her busy schedule.

Convenience has also played a huge role when it comes to the restaurant and packaged-food industry. According to the NPD Group, Millennials are more likely than earlier generations to use convenience foods including frozen meals and other food preparation options that require minimal preparation.[21] Although many Millennials are willing to accept lower-quality products in exchange for convenience and price, they are not ready to throw quality completely out the window. *Consumer Reports* indicates that quality is now more important to Millennials when they consider fast-food options than it was in 2011.[22] This has forced many companies to rethink their brands so that convenience and quality work together to entice Millennial shoppers.

One brand that has taken this to heart and completely restructured itself to appeal to this new, Millennial-inspired trend is Domino's. Millennials old and young have a stronger affinity for pizza than most other generations. A 2012 report by Technomic indicated that four in ten consumers polled eat pizza once a week.[23] This is attributed largely to the convenience factor associated with ordering a pizza. Domino's was once viewed as the cheap cardboard-like pizza that broke college students bought at 2 a.m., but soon even those college students were turning away from the brand. Instead of hiding these harsh critiques, Domino's embarked on a rebranding journey in 2008 that was focused on authenticity and transparency. The campaign featured a five-minute documentary that did not shy away from consumer dislike of the pizza. Instead, viewers were invited to share the experience and see firsthand what Domino's was doing to improve the taste and ingredients used in the production of each pie. Overall, this campaign resulted in increased sales and more brand loyalty than the brand had seen in the past. In 2011, Domino's shares rose 75 percent compared with just a 15 percent increase for Papa John's.[24] Through the entire rebranding process, Domino's maintained its original promise of thirty-minute delivery time, keeping it top of mind for consumers looking for a convenient quick meal. When considering Millennial parents, pizza may not be the first dinner choice that comes to mind, but imagine this scenario:

Julie is a Millennial mother hosting her 8-year-old daughter's six friends for a slumber party. She could spend hours in the kitchen making dinner for all seven children, but that would be such a hassle. Instead, she pulls out her phone and uses the new Domino's voice-ordering app. In minutes, Julie has ordered two large pizzas and plugged her order number into the online Pizza Tracker on the Domino's website. She sets her kids up with a movie and watches online as the tracker counts down the time until her order will show up at her door. Soon, the kids are gathered around her tablet, watching the tracker, too. In less than thirty minutes, everyone is happily eating their pizza and enjoying a fun evening, and Julie doesn't have to worry about washing a single dish.

Domino's is one of the brands that delivers on its promise of convenience. Powerful players in the restaurant industry are quickly realizing that this type of fast-service, convenient meal option is becoming more popular with one of the busiest generations to date. Millennials are constantly on the go, and they do not have the time to slow down for anything. When it comes to family entertainment, Millennial parents are looking for budget-friendly restaurants and dinner options that accommodate children but do not take up too much time.

Even convenience store shopping has seen a significant increase as a result of higher Millennial interest in convenience products. General Mills Convenience and Foodservice conducted a study in 2013 to gain insights about the Millennial convenience store shopper and found that, overall, Millennials are 53 percent more likely to shop at convenience stores than adults over the age of 35.[25] Life stage plays a huge role in the rate at which shoppers visit convenience stores; nonparent Millennials are more likely to run into a convenience store to make a last-minute purchase to tide them over for a couple of days, whereas a Millennial parent is more inclined to plan and shop for the week, since shopping with young children can be quite a hassle and running out to the store just for milk can sometimes be impossible.

In an era of Redbox movie rentals, food trucks, and e-commerce, convenience has been taken to a whole new level. The drive for convenience brands will not slow down anytime soon, especially as Millennials expand their families and take on new life roles.

Loyal to Loyalty Programs

How many times have you heard that Millennials aren't loyal, they're just looking for the best deal or the newest gadget with no regard for brand? This is just not true. Though Millennial parents are price oriented, they still value and are loyal to brands that fulfill their needs in a pragmatic way. Therefore, brands that offer the greatest amount of utility have the ability to charge a modest premium for their products or services. This is true specifically when it comes to Millennial moms. Though they stick to a tight budget when making a purchase, Millennial mothers are more willing to spend based on quality—especially when they are rewarded for their loyalty.

As the age-old saying goes, "The man may be the head of the household, but the woman is the neck and she can turn the head any way she wants." When striving to achieve household loyalty, smart brands are aiming to target Millennial moms who control the majority of household decisions related to the family's over-all well-being. Girl Power, a public relations and marketing con-sultancy that focuses specifically on marketing to the influential woman, found that U.S. moms have a buying power of $2.1 trillion and control close to 85 percent of the entire household income.[26] As Millennial women are becoming mothers at an increasing rate, their influence in the household is becoming an important factor for brands developing their new marketing messages.

How does this tie in to loyalty? Get a Millennial mom on your side, and you have a family who supports your brand and is loyal to your company. The key is how to get Millennial moms to become loyal and make repeat purchases. On average, 45 percent of Mil-lennial moms feel as though marketing campaigns are not directed toward them.[27] This provides a huge opportunity for brands that want to connect with this up-and-coming demographic. By creating individual messages and providing opportunities for moms to connect with each other, brands have the potential to tap into the Millennial partner model.

Moxie Jean, an online consignment store, helps moms get the best designer-brand clothing and goods for their little ones at an affordable price. The site has received extremely high awareness and positive reviews from Millennial moms, who claim the service is far beyond what they expected. Christine Wilson, founder and CEO of MtoM Consulting, an agency that specializes in marketing products and services to the "digital mom," works closely with Moxie Jean. Wilson explained in an interview that the traditional loyalty program does not relate to young Millennial parents. The focus at Moxie Jean is on improving the customer relationship with the brand to increase loyalty rather than creating a standard loyalty program that is dependent on the number of times you visit the store or on collecting points for every item bought. "We don't necessarily call it a loyalty program," Wilson says. "Our goal is to create an environment where the customer doesn't really realize they are a part of anything beyond just great service. We tailor every incentive we send to shoppers based on their previous shopping behavior." This allows Moxie Jean to create personalized messages, deals, and rewards for each shopper on the site. For example, if a customer is searching for girls' shoes in size four, the company will send her coupons and discounts for similar shoes while avoiding the discounts available for other, unrelated items. Essentially, Moxie Jean has created a system that is a loyalty program not in the way that a customer has to sign up for something but, rather, in a way that is based on customer relationship management and individualized and personalized communications. Moxie Jean's ultimate message is "We know you're a great customer, so we are giving you this reward without your even having to sign up for it."

In an era when brands need to be more transparent than ever and adopt authentic business models, Millennials will consistently require brands to work for their loyalty and acceptance. *What was once considered the best way to attract loyalty is now outdated and does not appeal to the Millennial Mindset.* At a tactical level, the role of loyalty programs has changed over time. Think about it this way: On your first date with someone new, your date brings you a box of chocolates. How lovely (and delicious!). This person must really be something. On your second date, the person brings you another box of chocolates. This is good—consistent and dependable, and who doesn't like that? On your third, fourth, and fifth dates, you keep getting the same box of chocolates. That's when you realize that consistency isn't doing it for you anymore. Now it's become predictable and boring—not to mention that your pants no longer fit because you've been eating so much chocolate.

This type of frequency or punch-card model, where, for example, you buy ten coffees and get one free, may create some repeat business, but it is not the same as brand loyalty or brand love. It may not get customers to go out of their way to come to your business or encourage them to tell their friends. However, according to research conducted by Bond Brand Loyalty (formerly Maritz Loyalty Marketing), 37 percent of Millennials would not be loyal to a brand that did not have a loyalty program of some sort. Additionally, 68 percent of Millennials surveyed said they change where and when they make purchases in order to receive benefits, and an additional 60 percent

would switch brands pending desired incentives.[28] Successful loyalty programs should be both linear and nonlinear, transparent, and
authentic. The Starbucks loyalty program is a great example of what
brands are doing to not only interact with Millennials and Millennial parents but also inspire loyalty and repeat purchases.

The My Starbucks Rewards program is one of the most favored
loyalty programs among Millennial parents. Overall, Starbucks
has consistently won with Millennials, and Millennial parents are
no different when it comes to Starbucks. My Starbucks Rewards
combines digital with face-to-face interactions and offers personalized benefits and rewards to customers who utilize the app when in
the store. Starbucks registers are programmed to read bar codes on
smartphones that link to prepaid Starbucks cards, making it easy
and commonplace for customers to pay for their tall Skinny Vanilla
Lattes simply by flashing their smartphones. The genius part of
this program is that the push toward digital does not diminish the
personal interaction of going into Starbucks and engaging with the
baristas. More and more brands are adopting this type of hybrid
loyalty program that combines authentic interactions with digital
technology.

Successful loyalty programs also incorporate elements of surprise and delight into the campaign. Millennials are most loyal to
brands that make them feel special. What better way to do that than
by creating an elite club? Members of the club receive special benefits and exclusive access to products or services. A great way to generate the environment of exclusivity is to connect with consumers
using an exclusive platform. Snapchat is the perfect way to do that.
Unless you have been living under a rock, you know that Snapchat
has a slightly provocative background. However, since its creation

in 2011, Snapchat has seen exponential growth within the Millennial demographic. According to a Business Insider report, 760 million disappearing photos and videos are sent daily, and the number of stories shared through Snapchat increased by 100 percent in just two months in 2014. Taco Bell leveraged this popularity in its Snapchat campaign to let customers know the widely popular Beefy Crunch Burrito would be making its return to the Taco Bell menu. Taco Bell is not often associated with Millennial parents; however, it still has a strong hold on Image First and Against the Grain orbits. Against the Grain parents are the most likely to eat the food they want regardless of the calories. They often treat themselves to food that is not good for them and believe that fast food fits into their busy lifestyle. Similarly, Image First parents tend to prefer fast food to home cooking. This provides Taco Bell with a huge opportunity to connect with Millennial parents.

With this in mind, Taco Bell tweeted on April 30, 2013, "We're @Snapchat. Username: tacobell. Add us. We're sending our friends a secret announcement tomorrow! #shhh." Almost immediately after the tweet was sent, thousands of eager consumers added Taco Bell on Snapchat. The next day Taco Bell sent its new followers a snap of a Beefy Crunch Burrito with the new release date doodled on the picture. Just as the company expected, the secret was not kept for long. Everyone who received the snap began tweeting and posting about the "secret" announcement, creating user-generated energy through a shareable format. Taco Bell received extremely positive feedback for this creative announcement strategy. One of the primary reasons this was such a win for Taco Bell was the result of the surprise and delight elements of the campaign. Research shows that 55 percent of Millennials believe that receiving personalized product or service experiences is an important factor in a successful loyalty program.[29] According to the YouGov Brand Index, there was a jump in word-of-mouth (WOM) exposure for Taco Bell among Millennial parents from April 28 to May 2, 2013, after the Snapchat release. On April 28, Taco Bell had a WOM exposure score of 17.6 and on May 2 the score increased to 19.6. These insights were collected using a moving average of ten weeks. Although Taco Bell is not a Millennial parent–specific brand, it nevertheless interacts with Millennial parents based on common generational traits. Combine this with the fact that Millennials are more likely to prefer nonmonetary loyalty brand benefits compared with the general population, and it is no surprise that Taco Bell won over so many Millennials with its Snapchat success. Ultimately, the best loyalty programs combine elements of both the traditional linear rewards programs and the nonlinear surprise and delight qualities.

A huge benefit of loyalty programs is the ability to collect consumer data, which allows organizations to analyze and understand their customers' shopping habits, likes, and dislikes, and truly personalizes the experience. However, this type of Big Data often becomes overwhelming for organizations and ends up sitting on a cloud (or in a cloud, we're not exactly sure how that works, but we know there is a cloud involved). Brands that sit on their Big Data and don't leverage it to create a better customer experience are

BEST-IN-CLASS LOYALTY PROGRAMS SHOULD BE

Linear - Providing expected benefits they can count on.
Nonlinear - Providing unexpected "surprise and delight" benefits to keep the relationship fresh.
Transparent - Not giving them a reason to question your motives or intent to reward their loyalty.
Authentic - The program should remain within your core brand authority.

missing the mark. When used correctly, Big Data can enable brands to create predictive analytics based on the spending patterns of the most loyal customers. This has the potential to provide key insights about product use, rate of purchase, and how often a customer comes into the store. Unstructured data includes everything from online browsing patterns to social media posts to mobile device locations to loyalty program participation to search habits to e-mail. If used correctly, the information available from this data provides brands with the opportunity to create customized shopping experiences and targeted loyalty programs. Essentially, Big Data provides brands with an understanding of the motivations behind consumer shopping preferences.

Millennials are ripe for programs that collect this type of data because, as a whole, they are more likely to share personal information with brands if they receive benefits. According to a survey conducted by the University of Southern California Annenberg Center for the Digital Future and Bovitz Inc., 51 percent of Millennials are willing to trade personal information as long as they get something in return.[30] In general, brands have the opportunity to gain huge amounts of information about their customers through their loyalty programs. The Millennial mom of today (and tomorrow) is also redefining privacy. She's far less concerned about privacy and sharing information on the Internet than she used to be. When it comes to sharing photos online, a recent BabyCenter survey found that only 15 percent of Millennial moms are somewhat or very concerned about posting photos of themselves compared to 25 percent of Gen X moms. (They are more concerned when it comes to sharing pictures of their kids—34 percent of Millennial moms and 43 percent of Gen X moms have some concerns about that.)[31] They are not only willing to share (or in some cases, overshare—we all know those moms) photos and stories among friends and families, but are willing to share personal information with brands when the perks are right.

The CVS ExtraCare program is a great example of a brand that is using customer data to create targeted loyalty benefits for each customer. The program allows shoppers to save money and earn rewards on almost everything they buy—not to mention that it gives them access to coupons that are determined based on the customers' purchase patterns. Each CVS Pharmacy has a red kiosk where shoppers can scan their ExtraCare shopper cards and instantly receive the most relevant and useful coupons according to their spending habits. Not only does this create a customized experience for shoppers, but it also encourages them to make a purchase during their current trip. We've all been to a grocery or convenience store that printed the next week's coupons on the receipt. I don't know about you, but that receipt almost always gets thrown out the moment I get home—who wants to hold on to a ten-foot piece of paper for a whole week? Millennial parents sure don't. The CVS program allows them to save time clipping coupons and looking on the Internet for deals and instead instantly gives them exactly what they are looking for in the store. Essentially, the program provides Millennial parents with their benefits before they begin shopping, creating instant gratification and a greater motivation to make a purchase. For a busy mom on the go, this is an ideal way to shop and get everything she needs in one visit.

Despite what some marketing professionals may argue, loyalty programs are not dying. They are simply evolving as shopper attitudes evolve—fueled mostly by the Millennial generation. The key to creating a successful loyalty program is not just generating awareness but creating purposeful interactions that drive shoppers back to your brand. Rethink the punch-card days of yore, and jump on board with the interactive loyalty programs that are winning over the most influential Millennial shoppers.

CHAPTER 5: KEY TAKEAWAYS

⊃ **Brand love trumps brand awareness.** The new model for measuring brand affinity now includes participative benefits. This means that awareness of a brand is no longer enough to drive traffic and purchases—it is the price of admission to win but not a guarantee. Engagement with Millennials is key and allows them to create a stronger connection with the brand that influences loyalty and repeat customers. By creating Millennial partners, rather than Millennial targets, brands are more likely to create an authentic relationship with Millennials that makes them feel valued and includes them in the creation process, strengthening their brand love and affinity for a company.

⊃ **Price + quality + convenience = a win.** Millennials, especially parents, are price driven but they are not willing to compromise the quality of products that affect the well-being of the family. This is especially true in the grocery, technology, and automobile industries. By creating a business model that combines price, quality, and convenience (like Walmart has done), brands have a better chance of winning Millennial Mindset customers and creating lasting relationships. Offering promotions and limited-time offers also gamifies the shopping experience and connects specifically with the Millennial mom.

⊃ **Millennials are loyal—but you have to earn it.** Loyalty is not a given with Millennials, but it can be earned by brands that are authentic, are transparent, and align with their values and beliefs. Traditional loyalty programs have been upgraded and now must be both linear and nonlinear to get the most traction. Millennials want to connect with brands that are able to combine digital with personalized benefits and face-to-face interactions, like the successful My Starbucks Rewards program.

CHAPTER 6

Spotlight on Millennial Dads

We hope that you are taking a moment to pat yourself on the back, not only for finishing the whole book (assuming you didn't just skip to the last chapter . . . tsk, tsk, tsk), but for taking the initiative to learn more about the Millennials of today and tomorrow.

Throughout this book we've highlighted key trends that are influenced by Millennial parents and the brands that are getting it right and the brands that are getting it not-so-right. And you are probably walking away with some great thought starters led by data on Millennials, and Millennial moms in particular. But simple math tells us that is only the half the story. What about Millennial dads? Aren't they important to marketers? And why do they get only this stinkin' chapter, while Millennial moms get the majority of this book?

You've asked great questions throughout this book, and this is no exception. Millennial dads are important, and they are different from our fathers and our father's fathers. While Mom still has the greatest spending power overall, the role of Dad and the impact of his influence in the household is different than ever before, and in a very exciting way! Millennial men who have taken on the role of dad are redefining what that means and completely changing the way brands speak to young fathers.

Dad's New Role

When Bryan's wife, Danielle, was offered a job after several years of unemployment as a result of being laid off, the two had to discuss the pros and cons of her returning to work. Did we mention that during the years Danielle was not working, they expanded their family and now have three beautiful young children? The job offer required them to evaluate their earning potential vs. the contributions each of them made to child rearing and household maintenance. The decision didn't linger on who would be best suited to taking care of the children, but, as with so many Millennials feeling the economic pinch, it came down to dollars and cents—and sense.

The U.S. Census Bureau defines a stay-at-home dad as "a married father with children under 15 years old who has remained out of the labor force for more than one year primarily so he can care for his family while his wife works outside the home." The Census Bureau estimates that there were 189,000 stay-at-home dads as of 2012.[1] But wait—that definition seems awfully limiting. What about dads who are freelancers or work part-time from home? Dads who aren't married? Those who have a wife who goes to school or works from home? Beth Latshaw, an assistant professor of sociology at Appalachian State University, estimates that there were closer to 1.4 million stay-at-home dads as of 2009, based on a broader and more realistic definition of the term as married fathers of children under age 18 who work less than twenty-five hours a week and have a spouse who works thirty or more hours a week.[2] The National At-Home Dad Network has adopted this new estimate as the most accurate.

As the number of stay-at-home dads increases, it is becoming more and more evident that Millennials are leaving their mark on more than just the economy—they are reshaping the way our society views parenthood. Millennial dads want to be present for the upbringing of their children, and they want to contribute more than just financial security. Nathan, a 24-year-old Millennial, is not yet a father, but he hopes to start a family in the next five to eight years. Although he intends to keep a steady job throughout his career, he believes that the traditional gender roles for parents are archaic. "I think that the Archie Bunker mentality of home life is outdated. Women should be helping out financially as much as men should be helping to raise kids, and [do] the daily house activities," Nathan says. He explains that he wants to be attentive to his family's needs and help with child care any way he can.

Nathan is not the only Millennial man who has this opinion. A recent Edelman survey found that 82 percent of first-time fathers feel that they share the child care responsibilities evenly—creating a partnership method of parenting instead of the traditional divided roles.[3] Despite the stereotypes, Millennial men are enthusiastic about starting a family. Sure, they still want the Benz or the Bentley, but many believe that fatherhood is the supreme symbol of masculinity. Not only are these young men wholeheartedly stepping into their new roles, they are also redefining what it means to be a father.

Dads Are Snowflakes, Too

Just like Millennial parents as a group, there are different types of dads out there, and it's important for marketers to distinguish among them. CEB Iconoculture recently conducted a behavioral segmentation study to identify four segments of fathers, focusing on habits, behaviors, and psychographics/attitudes of dads.

- **Provider dad.** This traditional father shows his love by providing for his family and taking care of the "manly chores" around the house.

- **Blender dad.** Taking on more responsibility with the kids and the house, this dad is sharing the load or is a single parent or part of a blended family.

- **Socializer dad.** This dad is all about creativity and balance, constantly keeping busy physically and socially.

- **Achiever dad.** Having prioritized education and affluence in his own life, he imparts those values to his children as well.[4]

Can you guess which two of these segments are more concentrated within the Millennial demographic? Go ahead, we'll wait.

You guessed it! Forty percent of Socializer dads are Millennials, and 38 percent of Achiever dads are Millennials. The drive for personal connections does not stop with moms. Dads are actively seeking out recommendations, opinions, and ideas from their friends in various social networks.

As we mentioned earlier, Millennial moms see themselves as more fun and relaxed than their Baby Boomer parents. This trend is true among Millennial dads as well: Both the Socializer dad and the Achiever dad value creativity and fun. It is also important to note that within both of these populations Dad wants to maintain his own personal identity separate from being a father. Unlike their Boomer predecessors, Millennial dads are struggling to accept some of the new challenges fatherhood brings. Although they agree that having a child brings them happiness and has been one of the most rewarding experiences of their lives, being a father has affected their sense of self. According to research conducted by DDB, 25 percent of Millennials agreed with the statement "I've lost my identity because I am a dad." We get that this may seem a little pessimistic, but this provides a great opportunity for new brands to foster relationships that help young fathers maintain their individual sense of self in addition to being a father.

Sense of self-identity is an overall strong Millennial value, but Millennial men are especially aware of the way other people see them. They are concerned with their self-image and want their favorite brands to reflect their personal identity. This represents a major shift in male shopping trends from previous generations. Men from the Boomer generation were less concerned with fashion while in their prime and, instead, focused more on traditional responsibilities. Today, 38 percent of Millennial men define themselves as fashionable and trendy (compared to only 16 percent of Boomer men).[5] The key is to combine the desire to be fashionable with the desire to be a good father. Combine both of these traits, and you have a product that is both shareworthy and unique.

Help Dad Be Great

With the changing role of Dad, you would think that marketers target men as decision makers or influencers for household products, showing them as modern dads. You would be very wrong. Professors Jim Gentry and Robert Harrison conducted a study of almost 1,400 commercials during sporting events between 2007 and 2009 and established that men were virtually never shown in a positive family light. In fact, less than 2 percent of commercials showed men in a domestic role or having an emotional connection to their children. A small percentage of commercials showed men shopping, but only for "manly" products, like beer or auto parts.[6]

Google Chrome, however, changed the status quo and connected with dads in a whole new way in its "Dear Sophie" spot that aired in 2011. The campaign was based on a computer screen, showing a new account being created for a newborn girl, Sophie. The first e-mail says, "You arrived," with a picture of the baby attached. Subsequent posts hit on other milestones in this little girl's life, including her first birthday, riding a bike, a ballet recital, and falling down while skiing. There are some clues throughout the commercial as to who set up this account, but you don't really know until the end, when this message is displayed: "I've been writing you since you were born. I can't wait to share this with you someday. Love, Dad." Hold on a moment, I think I've got something in my eye . . .

Once you've composed yourself, too, let's talk about why this is a great ad, not only in the way it portrays Dad but also in targeting Millennials. This spot portrays Dad as a real person who is green when it comes to dealing with a baby ("I'm still getting the hang of holding you") but is also overwhelmed with love and emotion. An e-mail video of the little girl crying in terror as she rides a toy train has the caption "This was Mom's idea." Typical dad joke. With each e-mail, another feature of Google Chrome is seamlessly shown—attaching pictures, videos, web albums, and Google Earth links. This is such a powerful commercial for so many reasons. Watching a child growing up and capturing those milestones and feelings along the way is touching, to say the least. Google Chrome can help you do it in a way that integrates seamlessly into your life—it's as easy as sending an e-mail.

Even though men and women are different (Mars and Venus, as you well know), do marketers always have to single men out and market to them separately? Not always. At the 2014 Dad 2.0 Summit, marketers, thought influencers, and bloggers came together to discuss the changing role of dads and our modern perceptions of fatherhood. One of the greatest lessons to come out of the summit was the power of portraying the "real" family. What some brands don't understand is that by targeting either Mom *or* Dad, they are missing out on the other one. The panel discussion "Marketing to Today's Man" was conducted by thought leaders in the male marketing space, all of whom agreed that advertising to parents should be inclusive. Their research showed that women want their husbands portrayed properly and rank a brand higher if the ad shows an engaged father.[7] Essentially, keep Dad happy by including him in the family picture and adding to his self-confidence, keep Mom happy by showing her husband as a good father, and you have a winning ad for both parents.

Tag, You're It

Marketing is a fluid industry—there is no option for stagnation when it comes to engagement strategies. As customers change, marketing models change with them. Millennials were once young consumers who were only interested in themselves and what they could get out of the world. Now they are parents. They have responsibilities, families, careers, and a new view of the world that is founded on pragmatism. Millennial moms and dads alike are a new generation of parents that not only require but also *expect* brands to reach out to them in ways that are innovative, interactive, and engaging. We've provided you with the tools you need to make it out there in this new participation economy. Now it's your turn to show us you can do it.

AFTERWORD

Millennials with kids are the most informed, digitally savvy, innovative, and pragmatic parents in history. Their beliefs and behaviors are far different from those of previous generations, and they will shape the near future of our economy.

This journey started more than five years ago, when our leadership team set out to make Barkley the most informed marketing agency in America as it relates to Millennials. Our goal was to uncover insights that would allow us to help our clients prepare their brands for the future. Jeff Fromm became our champion.

He started by forming partnerships with Boston Consulting Group and Service Management Group to conduct the largest-scale research study to date on the Millennial generation as consumers. The initial research resulted in one of the first comprehensive reports about the Millennial generation: "American Millennials: Deciphering the Enigma Generation."

This report fueled so much interest that Jeff decided to expand on the topic and coauthored our first book in 2013, *Marketing to Millennials*. The book highlighted our joint research plus a deeper segmentation exercise, uncovering five distinct groups within the

Millennial generation: Hip-ennial, Old-School Millennial, Clean-and-Green Millennial, Gadget Guru, and Millennial Mom.

It was this fifth group—Millennial Moms—that became the inspiration for further research and analysis that ultimately led to this book. We wanted to find out how Millennial men and women would change as a result of parenthood. Who were these new parents? Would having children affect their consumption? How would kids change the way they interacted with brands? How would their values change. And what kind of parents would they be?

We have answered these questions and dozens more in our second comprehensive book, *Millennials with Kids*.

The insights captured here are a reflection of Jeff's and Marissa's incredible work ethic, desire to learn, and ability to create important partnerships. From personal one-on-one interviews to big brand case studies, this book relays a narrative that paints a clear and descriptive picture of the youngest generation of parents in the United States. It is a must-read for anyone helping to steward a brand into the future.

Jeff King
CEO, Barkley

NOTES

Introduction

1. Jacqueline Doherty, "On the Rise," Barron's, April 29, 2013, http://online
   .barrons.com/article/SB50001424052748703889404578440972842742076
   .html#articleTabs_article%3D1.

Chapter 1: Who Are They Now?

1. "Millennials in Adulthood," Pew Research Center, March 7, 2014, http://www
   .pewsocialtrends.org/2014/03/07/millennials-in-adulthood/.
2. David Gutting and Jeff Fromm, "Millennials as New Parents: The Rise of a
   New American Pragmatism," Barkley/FutureCast, 2013.
3. Joyce A. Martin, M.P.H.; Brady E. Hamilton, Ph.D.; Michelle J. K. Osterman,
   M.H.S.; Sally C. Curtin, M.A.; and T. J. Mathews, M.S., "Births: Final Data
   for 2012," National Vital Statistics Reports, December 30, 2013, http://www.cdc
   .gov/nchs/data/nvsr/nvsr62/nvsr62_09.pdf.
4. Jennifer Ludden and Brad Wilcox, "Young Families Delay Marriage, Not Parenthood," *Talk of the Nation*, NPR, December, 6, 2010, http://www.npr.org/2010/
   12/06/131853955/young-families-delay-marriage-not-parenthood.
5. Wendy Wang and Paul Taylor, "For Millennials, Parenthood Trumps Marriage,"
   Pew Research, March 9, 2011, http://www.pewsocialtrends.org/2011/03/09/
   for-millennials-parenthood-trumps-marriage.
6. Kay S. Hymowitz, "The Truth About Marriage in America," Manhattan Institute for Policy Research, December 16, 2011, http://www.manhattan-institute
   .org/html/miarticle.htm?id=7728#.UwDbtfldUYO.
7. Elena Weinstein, "Life Style Study on Millennial vs. Boomer Dads," DDB,

June 15, 2012, http://www.ddb.com/blog/community/life-style-study-on
-millennial/.

8. Wendy Wang, Kim Parker, and Paul Taylor, "Breadwinner Moms: Mothers Are
the Sole or Primary Provider in Four-in-Ten Households with Children; Public
Conflicted About the Growing Trend," Pew Research, May 29, 2013, http://
www.pewsocialtrends.org/2013/05/29/breadwinner-moms/#fn-17132–1.

9. "Confidence in Institutions," Gallup, June 2014, http://www.gallup.com/poll/
1597/confidence-institutions.aspx.

Chapter 2: Welcome to the Ization Nation

1. Mr Youth and RepNation Media, "Why Millennial Moms are Supplanting College Students as the Most Connected and Technology Dependent Population,"
Millennial Mom 1010, http://www.mryouth.com/Archives/millennialMom101
.pdf.

2. "Mr. and Mrs. Millennial Mom and Dad: An In-Depth Behavioral Segmentation Study of Millennials with Children," FutureCast, 2014.

3. "North American Consumer Technographics Retail Survey, 2014," Forrester,
May 2014.

4. Ibid.

5. Anthony M., Yelp review, October 20, 2013, http://www.yelp.com/biz/chipotle
-cultivate-festival-chicago.

6. BabyCenter 21st Century Mom® Insights Series, 2014 Millennial Mom Report, January 2014, http:www.babycentersolutions.com/docs/BabyCenter_2014
_Millennial_Mom_Report.pdf.

7. Ibid.

8. Weinstein, "Life Style Study on Millennial vs. Boomer Dads."

9. Larissa Faw, "Millennial Dads: Why Must We Make Sacrifices for Our
Kids?," Forbes, June 14, 2012, http://www.forbes.com/sites/larissafaw/2012/
06/14/millennial-dads-why-must-we-make-sacrifices-for-our-kids/.

10. Jeff Fromm, Celeste Lindell, and Lainie Decker, "American Millennials: Deciphering the Enigma Generation," Barkley/FutureCast, 2011.

11. Jeanette Nyberg, "Storybots App Review," Artchoo!, July 19, 2013, http://
artchoo.com/storybots-app-review/.

12. Justin Menza, "IKEA's Not Just for College Students: Exec," Consumer Nation,
October 1, 2012, http://www.cnbc.com/id/49241508.

13. Ikea Share Space, http://www.theshare-space.com.

14. Matt Carmichael, "As Millennials Get Nostalgic, Brands Can Take Advantage,"

AdAge, December 10, 2010, http://adage.com/article/adagestat/millennials
-nostalgic-brands-advantage/147601/.

15. Alex Knapp, "LeVar Burton On Reading Rainbow's Kickstarter and the Love
of Reading," Forbes, June 6, 2014, http://www.forbes.com/sites/alexknapp/
2014/06/06/levar-burton-on-reading-rainbows-kickstarter-and-the-love-of
-reading/.

16. Anjli Raval, "Record Income Gap Fuels U.S. Housing Weakness," Financial Times, August 12, 2014, http://www.ft.com/intl/cms/s/0/1b294ed0-222b
-11e4-9d4a-00144feabdc0.html#axzz3JuTv5DsR.

17. Emily Hefter, "Sean Could Buy a Condo, but He'd Rather Live in a Mansion
with 9 Roommates," Zillow, August 13, 2014, http://www.zillow.com/blog/
millennials-not-eager-to-buy-157461.

18. Amy Hoak, "Your Kids Decide When You Buy a Home," Market Watch,
May 20, 2104, http://www.marketwatch.com/story/your-kids-decide-when
-you-buy-a-home-2014-05-20.

19. Paul Taylor, "More Than Half of Millennials Have Shared a 'Selfie,'" Pew
Research Center, March 4, 2014, http://www.pewresearch.org/fact-tank/
2014/03/04/more-than-half-of-millennials-have-shared-a-selfie/.

20. Ryan Mac, "The Mad Billionaire Behind GoPro: The World's Hottest Camera Company," Forbes, March 4, 2013, http://www.forbes.com/sites/ryanmac/
2013/03/04/the-mad-billionaire-behind-gopro-the-worlds-hottest
-camera-company/.

21. http://gopro.com/.

22. "Mothers and Daughters: The Working Mother Generations Report," Working
Mother Research Institute, 2014, http://www.wmmsurveys.com/Generations
_Report.pdf.

Chapter 3: Fifty Shades of Your Brand

1. George Winslow, "New York Times Report: One Third of Millennials Watch
No Broadcast TV," Broadcasting & Cable, October 10, 2103, http://www.broad
castingcable.com/news/technology/ny-times-report-one-third-millennials
-watch-no-broadcast-tv/123907.

2. Todd Spangler, "Netflix Keeps Up Growth Spurt, Adding 4 Million Subscribers in Q1," Variety, April 21, 2014, http://variety.com/2014/digital/news/netflix
-keeps-up-growth-spurt-adding-4-million-subscribers-in-q1-1201160207.

3. Richard Verrier, "DreamWorks Animation to Unveil First Original Series for
Netflix," Los Angeles Times, December 24, 2013, http://www.latimes.com/

entertainment/envelope/cotown/la-et-ct-dreamworks-animation-netflix
-turbo-fast-20131224-story.html#page=1.

4. BabyCenter 21st Century Mom® Insights Series, 2014 Millennial Mom Report.

5. Fromm, Lindell, and Decker, "American Millennials: Deciphering the Enigma Generation."

6. Weber Shandwick and KRC Research, "Digital Women Influencers: Millennial Moms," http://www.webershandwick.com/uploads/news/files/millennialMoms _ExecSummary.pdf.

7. Michael Carney, "Updates to Grocery iQ App Keep Coupons.com Atop the Mobile Couponing Mountain," Pandodaily, May 9, 2012, http://pando .com/2012/05/09/updates-to-grocery-iq-app-keep-coupons-com-atop-the -mobile-couponing-mountain/.

8. Zach Bulygo, "How Mint Grew to 1.5 Million Users and Sold for $170 Million in Just 2 Years," 2013, KISSmetrics, http://blog.kissmetrics.com/how-mint -grew/.

9. Ibid.

10. Babies and Toddlers Should Learn from Play, Not Screens," American Academy of Pediaraics, October, 18, 2011, http://www2.aap.org/pressroom/mediaunder2.pdf.

11. F. J. Zimmerman, D. A. Christakis, and A. N. Meltzoff, "Television and DVD/ Video Viewing in Children Younger Than 2 Years," Archives of Pediatrics and Adolescent Medicine, May 2007.

12. Amazon product reviews, http://www.amazon.com/Fisher-Price-Ipad-Apptivity -Seat-Newborn-to-Toddler/dp/B00EL4NI5U/ref=sr_1_1?ie=UTF8&qid=139 6104285&sr=8-1&keywords=apptivity+seat.

13. Truman Lewis, "Petitions Demand Recall of Fisher-Price 'Apptivity Seat for iPad,'" Consumer Affairs, December 20, 2013, http://www.consumeraffairs .com/news/petitions-demand-recall-of-fisher-price-apptivity-seat-for-ipad -122013.html.

Chapter 4: The Power of Energy

1. BabyCenter 21st Century Mom® Insights Series, 2014 Millennial Mom Report.

2. Ibid.

3. Claire Suddath, "The Millennial Way of Shopping: More Careful, Durable, and Frugal Than You Think," BusinessWeek, http://www.businessweek.com/ articles/2014-04-25/millennials-are-careful-frugal-shoppers-who-buy-for-the -long-term.

4. Coca-Cola Content 2020 Part One, https://www.youtube.com/watch?v=Lerd MmWjU_E.

5. "Home Buyer and Seller Generational Trends," 2014 National Association of Realtors®, March 2014, http://www.realtor.org/sites/default/files/reports/2014/2014-home-buyer-and-seller-generational-trends-report-full.pdf.

6. MINDDRIVE About page, http://minddrive.org/about/.

7. Fred Bauters, "At-Risk Students' Electric Car Makes It from KC to D.C. on "Social Fuel," Silicon Prairie News, June 7, 2013, http://www.siliconprairienews .com/2013/06/at-risk-students-electric-car-makes-it-from-kc-to-d-c-on-social -fuel.

8. Dian Schaffhauser, "Millennial Parents: Schools Could Do Better Teaching Tech," The Journal, July 29, 2014, http://thejournal.com/articles/2014/07/29/ millennial-parents-schools-could-do-better-teaching-tech.aspx.

9. David Erickson and Martin van der Roest, "Optimizing Content Creation for Generational Marketing," September 11, 2013, Interview #18 Transcript, http://cmexaminer.cadence9.com/transcripts/optimizing-content-creation-for -generational-marketing.

10. BabyCenter 21st Century Mom® Insights Series, 2014 Millennial Mom Report.

11. Daniel Roberts, "Drew Brees Talks Endorsement Deals," Fortune, February 1, 2013, http://fortune.com/2013/02/01/drew-brees-talks-endorsement-deals/.

Chapter 5: The Middle of the Road Could Be the End

1. "Financial Capability in the United States," FINRA Investor Education Foundation, May 2013, http://www.usfinancialcapability.org/downloads/NFCS_2012 _Report_Natl_Findings.pdf.

2. Carolo de Bassa Schereburg, "College-Educated Millennials: An Overview of Their Personal Finances," Teachers Insurance and Annuity Association of America, February 2014, https://www.tiaa-crefinstitute.org/public/pdf/gflec_overview _millennials_personal_finances_feb2014.pdf.

3. Gutting and Fromm, "Millennials as New Parents."

4. BabyCenter 21st Century Mom® Insights Series, 2014 Millennial Mom Report.

5. Fromm, Lindell, and Decker, "American Millennials."

6. BabyCenter 21st Century Mom® Insights Series, 2014 Millennial Mom Report.

7. "Millennials Embrace High-Low Budgeting," Ypulse, January 6, 2013, http:// www.ypulse.com/post/view/millennials-display-high-low-budgeting-habits.

8. Gutting and Fromm, "Millennials as New Parents."

9. Chanelle Bessette, "Social Media Superstars 2014," Fortune, January 16, 2014, http://fortune.com/2014/01/16/social-media-superstars-2014-fortunes-best-companies-to-work-for/.

10. Gutting and Fromm, "Millennials as New Parents."

11. Fromm, Lindell, and Decker, "American Millennials."

12. Larissa Faw, "Why Millennials Are Spending More Than They Earn, and Parents Are Footing the Bill," Forbes, May 18, 2012, http://www.forbes.com/sites/larissafaw/2012/05/18/why-millennials-are-spending-more-than-they-earn/.

13. Gutting and Fromm, "Millennials as New Parents."

14. Mickey Ristroph, "Are Self-Checkouts Paving the Way for a New Commerce Experience?," Mobile Marketer, May 12, 2014, http://www.mobilemarketer.com/cms/opinion/columns/17782.html.

15. Frank Levy and Richard J. Murnane, "Dancing with Robots: Human Skills for Computerized Work," Third Way, 2013, http://content.thirdway.org/publications/714/Dancing-With-Robots.pdf.

16. Robert Rizzuto, "Big Y to Eliminate All Self Checkout Kiosks by End of Year," Mass Live, September 17, 2011, http://www.masslive.com/business-news/index.ssf/2011/09/big_y_to_eliminate_all_self-checkout_kio.html.

17. Teresa Novellino, "Zulily Flexed Its Flash-Site Muscle as IPO Took Off," Upstart Business Journal, November 15, 2013, http://upstart.bizjournals.com/money/loot/2013/11/15/zulily-goes-public-in-flash-model-test.html.

18. Zulily About us page, http://www.zulily.com/about-us.

19. Angel Gonzalez, "Zulily: Hot Site for Moms Hits a Moment of Truth," Seattle Times, February 21, 2014, http://seattletimes.com/html/businesstechnology/2022957853_zulilyfeaturexml.html.

20. John Cook, "Daily Deal Site Zulily Raises $43 Million at Huge Valuation of More Than $700 Million," GeekWire, August 10, 2011, http://www.geekwire.com/2011/daily-deal-site-zulily-raises-43-million-huge-valuation-700-million.

21. "Cravings, Cost Control, and Minimal Preparation Drive the Millennial Generation's Food Choices, Reports NPD," NPD Group, August 11, 2010, https://www.npd.com/wps/portal/npd/us/news/press-releases/pr_100811/.

22. "Best and Worst Fast-Food Restaurants in America," Consumer Reports, July 2014, http://www.consumerreports.org/cro/magazine/2014/08/best-and-worst-fast-food-restaurants-in-america/index.htm.

23. Domenick Celentano, "Technomic Pizza Consumer Trend Report: Fast Casual and Upscale QSR Driving Market Growth," http://foodbeverage.about.com/od/Whats_Hot/a/Technomic-Pizza-Consumer-Trend-Report-Tasty-Food-Trends-2012.htm.

24. Anna-Louise Jackson and Anthony Feld, "Domino's 'Brutally Honest' Ads Attract Sales as Consumer Spending Falters," Bloomberg, October 17, 2011, http://www.bloomberg.com/news/2011–10–17/domino-s-brutally-honest-ads -offset-slowing-consumer-spending.html.

25. "A View of Millennial Convenience Store Shoppers," General Mills Convenience and FoodService, January 2013, http://www.generalmillscf.com/ industries/convenience/support-tool-categories/consumer-insights/a-view-of -millennial-convenience-store-shoppers.

26. "Understanding the Mom Market," Girl Power Marketing, http://www.girl powermarketing.com/marketing_moms.html.

27. "Millennial Moms: The Untapped Opportunity," PunchTab, http://engagement .punchtab.com/millennial-moms-infographic.

28. "The Loyalty Report," Bond Brand Loyalty, 2014, http://cdn2.hubspot.net/ hub/352767/file-942578460-pdf/Whitepapers/Bond_Brand_Loyalty_2014 _Loyalty_Report_US.pdf?t=1407525211146.

29. Ibid.

30. "Is Online Privacy Over?," University of Southern California Annenberg Center for the Digital Future, April 22, 2013, http://annenberg.usc.edu/News%20 and%20Events/News/130422CDF_millennials.aspx.

31. BabyCenter 21st Century Mom® Insights Series, 2014 Millennial Mom Report.

Chapter 6: Spotlight on Millennial Dads

1. U.S. Census Bureau, "America's Families and Living Arrangements: 2012: Family Groups," Table FG8, Married Couple Family Groups with Children Under 15 by Stay-at-Home Status of Both Spouses: 2012, http://www.census.gov/ hhes/families/data/cps2012FG.html.

2. Beth Latshaw, "Qualitative Insights into Stay-at-Home Fatherhood," September 2009, http://paa2010.princeton.edu/papers/100462.

3. Maude Standish, "The Millennial Man Child Grows Up," Huff Post Business, June 20, 2013, http://www.huffingtonpost.com/maude-standish/the-millennial -man-child-grows-up_b_3461622.html.

4. Kate Muhl, Hans Eisenbeis, and Aaron Lotton, "D4: The Four Key Dads You Need to Know Now," CEB Iconoculture, August 2013, https://www.iconoculture .com/Media/PDF/pd_D4FourDadsPDF_377193_3.pdf.

5. Michelle Fenstermaker, Marketing and Men: Ignore Evolving Social Norms at Your Peril," Wayfind, Trends/Issue 09, http://wdwayfind.com/trends/marketing -and-men/.

6. James Gentry and Robert Harrison, "Is Advertising a Barrier to Male Movement Toward Gender Change?," Marketing Theory, March 2010, Volume 10, Number 74, http://homepages.wmich.edu/~r5harris/Documents/MarketingTheory.pdf.

7. Jeff Hay, "Marketing to Today's Men: Are Dads Leading the Way?," Dad 2.0 Summit, February 1, 2014, http://www.dad2summit.com/2014/02/01/marketing-to-todays-men-are-dads-leading-the-way/.

GLOSSARY

Brand Atom: The Brand Atom is a new approach to consumer engagement that includes partnership, intrigue, meaning, experience, and energy. Traditionally, the AIDA model worked in a linear pattern that focused on first building brand awareness, then sparking consumer interest, then creating consumer desire, and ultimately ending in a purchase. The Brand Atom model does not act in a linear way, nor are the pieces dependent on each other to function. The intrigue, meaning, and experience planets orbit around the energy nucleus. The entire model is connected by the partnership thread that acts as the force that keeps the pieces in motion. This model emphasizes that consumer engagement is a living and breathing entity that must be in motion and at work at all times.

Brand Partners: Millennials are a generation that expects to be completely involved in the entire brand journey. They want to cocreate the products they use, the messages they interact with, and the brands they love. It is time to reimagine the idea of a target audience and start to think about Millennials as your Brand Partners.

Brand Stand™: The Brand Stand is the foundation of every organization. The ultimate goal of a Brand Stand is to cultivate a message that goes beyond answering traditional brand positioning questions such as "What are my product's benefits?" and "How is my product different?" Instead, the Brand Stand answers the question "How do I treat everyone and everything around me?" Brand Stands inspire strategies that focus on Storyliving, Content Excellence, and conscious capitalism.

Casualization: The tendency of younger generations to make experiences that were traditionally considered formal more casual. For example, the practice of dressing up to travel by plane is no longer common among leisure travelers. Millennials have played a huge role in the modern casualization of our language. Texting shorthand, abbreviations, and hashtags are all examples of how Millennials have adapted and enhanced the casualization trend.

Conscious Capitalism: Conscious capitalism is more than just aligning yourself with a charity or philanthropic cause. Acting as a conscious capitalist is about standing for more than just your bottom line. It is understanding how your brand, your company, your organization, and your entire brand ecosystem bring value and add good to the community. Millennials believe they can truly make the world a better place and are more likely to interact with a brand that somehow makes that a reality.

Content Excellence: Traditionally, brands were focused on creative excellence. The idea was to create messages and then use a set of tried-and-true shotgun methodologies to get that message out to target audiences. Now marketing strategies that are founded in content see the most success with Millennial consumers. Content is the type of communication consumers choose to spend time with and acts as a vehicle through which dynamic stories are told.

Democratization: Millennials have inspired a new type of democracy that does not just apply to politics. Now, with the Internet integrated into our lives, nearly everyone has almost unlimited access to resources that would never have been available before. When applying the concept of democratization to marketing, the consumer ultimately has a say in almost all aspects of the economy—from the images we see to the messages we receive and the brands we interact with.

Millennial Brand Love™: Millennial Brand Love is a more relationship-driven model of determining brand value. The traditional equation to determine brand value was the sum of the emotional and functional benefits divided by the price. For Millennials, the brand value equation is the sum of the emotional, functional, *and* participative benefits divided by the total cost. This shows that in order to inspire and earn brand love, Millennials must feel included in every step of the brand journey. They want to cocreate the entire experience and participate with your brand in a way we have never seen before.

Millennial Cocreators: Cocreation is a very strong Millennial theme. As an interactive generation, Millennials believe that they should be included in the creation process when it comes to branded messages and products. Millennial cocreators are Millennials who want to interact with brands on a deeper level and have more interaction and engagement with brands during the entire brand journey—not just the final purchase phase.

Millennial Mindset™: Millennial Mindset consumers are shoppers who are not Millennials by definition but have adopted the mindset of a Millennial when it comes to purchasing habits and behaviors. For example, a 50-year-old man is not a Millennial but he still can be very aware and align with the health trend fueled predominantly by the Millennial generation.

Personalization: Personalization is a trend fueled by Millennials who seek out ways to express their personal identity. While participation is the consumer's ability to partner in the creation of a brand or product, personalization is the consumer's ability to customize a brand, product, or experience so that it is completely unique to that consumer. Millennials as new parents are now even personalizing their own parenting styles instead of relying on traditional methods that were considered the "normative" approach to parenting in the past.

Pragmatism: Pragmatism is a traditional American philosophy that approaches questions and life issues through a problem-solving perspective. As Millennials become parents, they are redefining what pragmatism means in terms of marketing and brand engagement. Millennial parents view brands through a pragmatic lens and will not interact or engage with a brand or product unless it adds some meaning or value to their lives and can help make their lives as parents easier and more efficient.

Storyliving™: The best and most successful brands embrace a culture of Storyliving in addition to storytelling. Millennials do not want to just hear what a brand has to say about its products or services in its brand messages; they want to see the story or the message being lived out. Essentially, Storyliving means brands must walk the walk and not just talk the talk.

Useful is the new cool™: For Millennials, innovative tech is not considered "cool" anymore. As digital natives, this generation grew up with innovative technology and expects brands to incorporate it into their products and messages. What is cool, however, is technology that is useful and can help make a Millennial's life easier. This concept "Useful is the new cool" can be applied to all categories ranging from consumer packaged goods (CPG) brands all the way to service-based mobile apps.

INDEX

ABOUT THE AUTHORS

Jeff Fromm is President of FutureCast, a marketing consultancy based in Kansas City, MO, that specializes in Millennial generation trends. He is also a regular contributor at Forbes.com and a frequent keynote speaker on marketing, consumer trends, and innovation. In 2011 he published his first landmark study about the Millennial generation through a research partnership with The Boston Consulting Group and Service Management Group, which ultimately led to the writing and publication of the book *Marketing to Millennials*. Jeff has more than 25 years of consulting experience across dozens of brands, from Build-A-Bear Workshop to Dunkin' Brands, and holds a degree in economics from The Wharton School of the University of Pennsylvania. Jeff began his informal research on Millennial trends in 1992, with the birth of his twin girls.

Contact him:
LinkedIn—Jeff Fromm
Twitter @jefffromm
Website: www.Millennialmarketing.com

Marissa Vidler is the founder of Clear Box Insights, a market research firm that creates a direct line of communication between consumers and executive leadership. With over 15 years of experience in research, and having personally spoken to thousands of consumers about their perceptions, lifestyles, and shopping behaviors, Marissa has witnessed the impact of Millennials becoming a major player in the market firsthand. On the cusp of Millennialhood herself, Marissa lives in Kansas City, MO, with her husband and three huskies.

Contact her:
LinkedIn—Marissa Vidler
Website: www.clearbox.com